SLEETMUTE

Stan Resnicoff

ISBN 978-0-6156-8771-1

9 8 7 6 5 4 3

For Nick Fogey

For Roger Smith

INTRODUCTION

1966. One summer job I had during my college years was driving a delivery truck for Friendship Dairies in New York City. Every night, from midnight to about 8 am, I drove my route in Manhattan, Brooklyn and Queens delivering about 50,000 pounds of cheese. It was a hard job but it paid well and at the end of the summer I was able to buy a brand new 650cc Triumph Bonneville motorcycle.

The bike was beautiful but it was my first bike and a bit much for me in New York City in those pre-helmet days and when a week later the bike was stolen, it probably saved my life.

Amazingly I had bought theft insurance and when I got my money back I went to visit my friend Richie Mishkin who that summer was working at the 79th Street Boat Basin. Who even knew there was a marina in Manhattan at that time? Anyway when I showed him that I had fourteen hundred dollar bills, he quickly snatched them out of my hand and just as quickly gave them to some guy and said to me, with a big smile on his face, "WE own a boat!"

And we did. It was a 1939 38 foot Matthews wood yacht. Since the only other boat I'd been on up to this point was a rowboat I was in shock (but fascinated). I also now had NO money left for rent or anything else so it looked like I was gonna be living on this boat, which also happened to be kind of illegal at the time.

My parents were so disappointed, but it turned out that living on the boat right there in Manhattan turned out to be an adventure and a half. It was a whole new set of experiences and inspirations, and it even seemed to help me do well in design school. It was better than great, it was exciting!

Except: during the winter, living right on the Hudson River, it was cold. Very very cold. Crying cold. Spring and summer more than made up for it but still, during those winters, I vowed that someday, if I could, I would never be cold again.......

PREFACE

I stared at the form. I was applying to VISTA (Volunteers in Service to America). I would be graduating in six months. It was 1968. I was 24. Vietnam. This might be a deferment.

---

7. SERVICE PREFERENCE

Note: While your preferences will be considered, VISTA will place Volunteers based on their individual talents and the needs of the requesting communities and organizations.

- ☐ NO PREFERENCE
- ☐ URBAN POVERTY AREA
- ☐ RURAL ASSIGNMENT
- ☐ NATIVE AMERICAN RESERVATION
- ☐ OTHER _____

I stared at the question. After years in New York I hated the cold. There was only one place I wanted to go. It was a fantasy but I was young and I thought I knew everything. I figured that if the federal government had VISTA in <u>any</u> state they had to have it in <u>every</u> state. I had nothing to lose. I wrote in big letters:

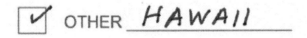

☑ OTHER _HAWAII_

I submitted the form.

PRATT INSTITUTE

THE TRUSTEES OF PRATT INSTITUTE, BY VIRTUE OF THE AUTHORITY
VESTED IN THEM, AND ON THE RECOMMENDATION OF THE FACULTY,
HAVE CONFERRED ON

STANLEY W. RESNICOFF

THE DEGREE OF

BACHELOR OF INDUSTRIAL DESIGN

FOR SATISFACTORY COMPLETION OF THE PRESCRIBED COURSE OF INSTRUCTION
IN EVIDENCE WHEREOF, THIS DIPLOMA HAS BEEN AWARDED
IN THE BOROUGH OF BROOKLYN, CITY OF NEW YORK,
JUNE SEVENTH, NINETEEN HUNDRED SIXTY-EIGHT.

James B. Donovan
PRESIDENT

CHAIRMAN, BOARD OF TRUSTEES

DEAN, SCHOOL OF ART AND DESIGN

I'VE GOT MAIL

I graduated three days ago.

I now had a Bachelor's Degree in Industrial Design from Pratt Institute in Brooklyn. Life was good.

I opened my mailbox. The first letter was from the Selective Service: U.S. Army. Inside were instructions on how and when to report to Fort Dix, New Jersey, and two subway tokens.

The second letter was from VISTA. I had been accepted into one of their programs.

Two letters. Both from the United States Government.

It was no contest.

Five days later I left for Alaska.

OBJECTIVES OF TRAINING

In order to work effectively in rural Alaska, the VISTA Volunteer must be prepared to:

1. Work cooperatively with individuals, informal groups, and the Council in the village to identify areas of need that can become a realistic focus of the Volunteer's efforts.

2. Appreciate local cultural, social, and political dynamics in developing his role and strategy.

3. Use initiative to begin a project when necessary to stimulate village response and participation in defining the Volunteer's goals and methods.

4. Using sensitivity to local responses, be prepared and able to alter the approach, the Volunteer's role, or the project itself as appropriate.

5. Assist individual members of the community to develop awareness and self-confidence to expand their own alternatives. with the subsequent objective that these individuals may be encouraged to do the same for their community, either as private activators or as VISTA Associates.

6. When villages are ready, assist individuals to build new structures or modify traditional structures to carry on the work of planning, implementing, and continually reassessing community or group goals.

7. Discover and help villagers employ the resources of agencies, organizations, and programs inside and outside the community in achieving their goals.

8. Use adequate measures to maintain personal health and safety in the Arctic environment.

9. Live where the people live, under similar economic and environmental limitations, learning as much as possible from them what is necessary to survive and get along.

10. Where there is a Village VISTA, use initiative to develop a working partnership with him to accomplish the objectives set out above, building on the unique perspectives and abilities of both parties.

11. Make constructive use of the guidance and support of the VISTA Project Development Officer in accomplishing the above goals.

12. Through research, evaluation, and participation in periodic conferences, assist the VISTA Supervisor and the Project Development Officers and fellow VISTAs in making the VISTA Alaska program as a whole increasingly relevant and effective.

13. Work within the guidelines and policies of VISTA National and VISTA Alaska.

TRAINING

Of course you don't get to Alaska just like that. It's the Government. First there are four weeks of training in Oregon.

I arrive. Me and my big duffel-bag. Now, I'm expecting that all the other kids in my group are gonna be like me: apprehensive about being sent to Alaska and really concerned with this 'cold' stuff. How wrong I was! Everybody's acting as if they've won the lottery. Found the Holy Grail. Alaska! Their eyes glossed over as they mouthed the word.

They also all seemed big. They talked about Eddie Bauer so much I thought he was one of the kids in the group. Some of them wore knives strapped to their legs. I realized that they all WANTED to go to Alaska. It was their fulfillment of a lifelong dream. I couldn't believe it.

We went through weeks of potentially meaningless 'community development' workshops. Not much said about Alaska. The Oregon police even had optional gun training. I didn't go because I wasn't planning to shoot anyone or anything. I kept my head low. My only objective was to survive training.

To add insult to injury, in the next room VISTA was training people to go to Hawaii. I could see them. They were all wearing shorts and those colored shirts. None of them had knives strapped to their legs. So close and yet so far.

Half the group didn't make it through training but those that did, including me, landed in Anchorage Alaska on July 24, 1968.

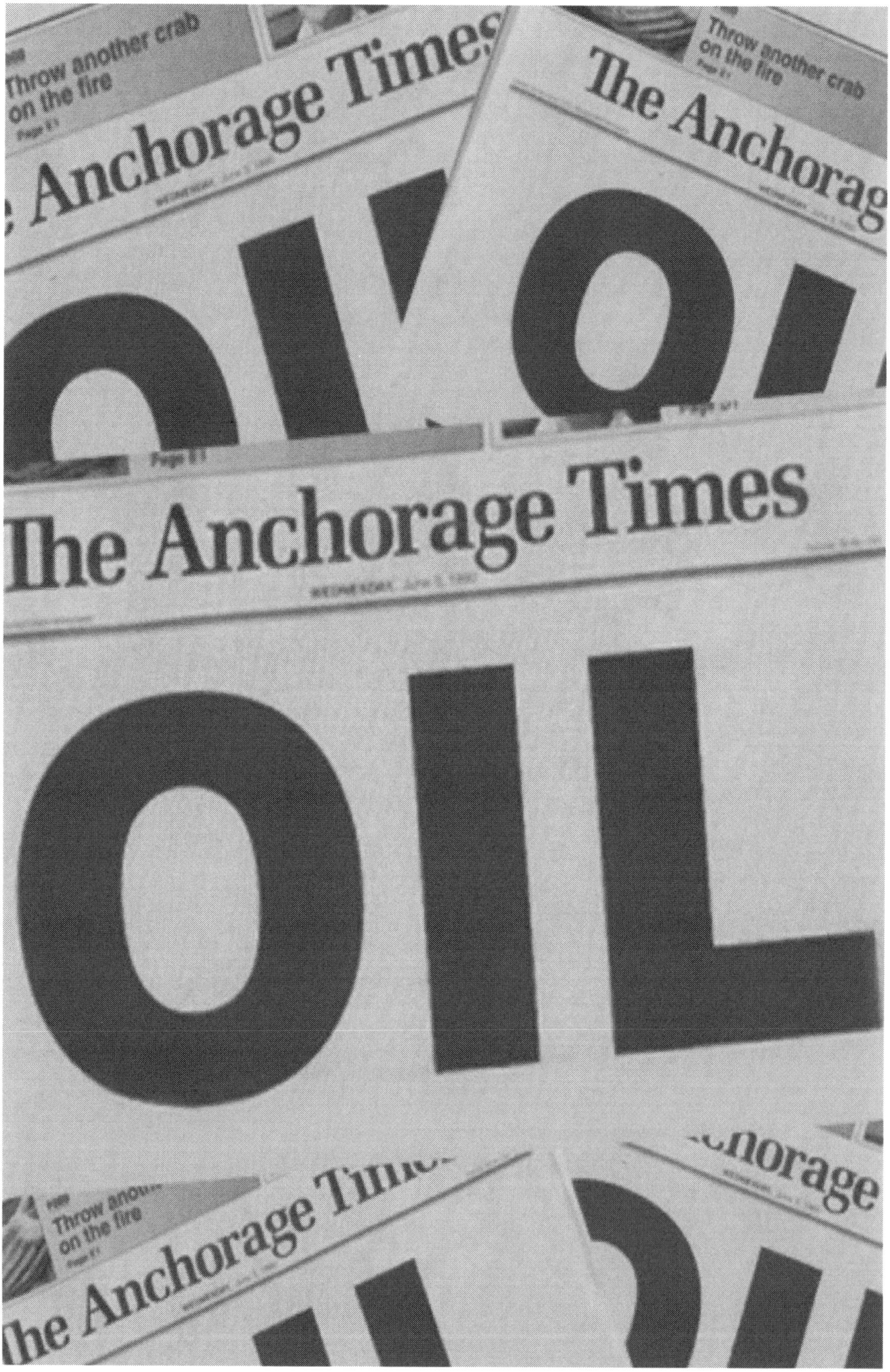
Throw another crab
on the fire
The Anchorage Times
OIL

OIL

The day we landed in Anchorage was the day they announced the discovery of oil in Alaska. The oil was nowhere near where I would wind up going, and had nothing to do with me but it was three pretty big letters for a newspaper headline.

GUNS

After we arrived in Anchorage VISTA gave us each 230 dollars to buy extra cold weather gear and supplies. I drifted around the stores. I came to a gun counter. VISTA kept saying that we might need to have a gun. Something about being out of the village picking berries and running onto a bear. It sounded unlikely to me. Besides, I knew nothing about guns.... except... staring me in the face was a shiny beautiful six-shooter – a cowboy gun – with it's revolving barrel, engraved leather gun belt and holster and, the piece-de resistance, the leather lace that ties around your thigh to hold your gun in place. Ooooooo.

In the conversation that followed I learned that I could, legally, buy this gun and wear it out on the street. Unbelievable. I paid the man, belted up, and walked out of the store into High Noon.

Now maybe people in Alaska had rifles or even had pistols with them but I was the only moron packin' a revolver (with leather thong) and walking around town like a gunfighter....arms slightly bowed....fingers twitching. Billy the Jew. I'm very lucky somebody didn't just shoot me as a public safety issue. They would not have been convicted. I was a major asshole.

VISTA was so disappointed in me. Not only did I blow my money but this gun was just the wrong thing to be wearing in an Eskimo village. Made you look like a lawman. They told me not to wear it when we entered the village. I said OK.

THE PROMISE

I felt that I was doing well in VISTA training and Alaska was more than interesting. Even Anchorage seemed like the frontier – the wild, wild west. It was, however, still summer and an Anchorage hotel room wasn't exactly an Eskimo village in winter at fifty below.

The Alaska VISTA trainers all seemed surprised if I mentioned in casual conversation that I hadn't applied to come to Alaska and that I wasn't particularly fond of the cold. I had to be careful about what I said because the trainers, as you would expect, treated Alaska not as a place, but as a religion. I still didn't want to be thrown out of the program, and like I said, Alaska <u>was</u> fascinating.

Anyway after some meetings and long-distance calls to VISTA headquarters it was proposed that I stay with the VISTA Alaska program for this year, and if I did well, VISTA would transfer me to Hawaii.

It wasn't what I wanted but I knew it was the best I was gonna get, so I 'enthusiastically' accepted.

CASWELL

Caswell cared. Caswell tried. He was big and strong, intelligent, sincere and a highly motivated volunteer. I didn't know it back then, but he didn't have a chance.

I met Caswell during Oregon training. We weren't friends because I kept my distance from all the other trainees. Caswell's moment of (unwanted) fame came during 'the drop-off'. This was a training game where VISTA rounded us up, without warning, and took away all our identification and money and sent us out alone into different rural villages in Oregon to survive for a weekend. Anyway Caswell somehow had gotten himself arrested and VISTA had to get him out of jail. In the end VISTA said that it was Caswell's enthusiasm that had gotten him into trouble (he was 'trying too hard') and the police had just locked him up 'for his own safety'. He remained in the program.

In Anchorage VISTA Alaska suggested that Caswell and I go to a village together. It was OK with both of us. When the village assignments were finally posted Resnicoff, S. and Caswell, P. were going to Sleetmute. Word was that it was a 'rough' smaller village on the Kuskoquim River. That was it.

I found out much later that VISTA was sure that I would quit as soon as the first cold hit (I guess I still spoke wistfully of Hawaii) and that Caswell would get into some kind of trouble because of his zealousness. They sent us to Sleetmute because Sleetmute was VISTA's lowest priority, hardly even a village in their eyes, and that when, not if, we both quit it would not embarrass the VISTA Alaska program. Probably no one would even know.

Me? I liked the sound of the name. Sleetmute.

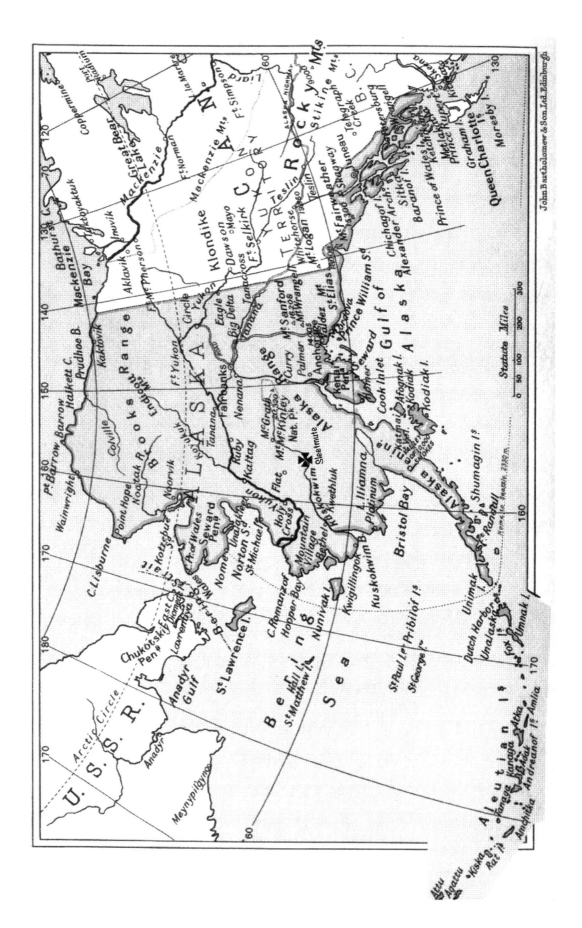

John Bartholomew & Son Ltd. Edinburgh

THE LAST LEG

It's been a long journey. New York City to Oregon to Anchorage to Bethel, Alaska. Tomorrow is the final leg...on to Sleetmute.

Morning. I want to look good so I put on my best shirt. We head down to the river where our bush pilot and his single-engine, four-seater Cessna is waiting for us. The plane is outfitted with pontoons. We'll be taking off and landing on the river. It's the pilot and me up front and Caswell and the VISTA trainer in the rear seats. The engine starts, we're racing down the river and after a moment we're in the air.

The view is incredible...skimming over the Kuskoquim River with forests and mountains for as far as you can see. I love flying.

Caswell promptly vomits all over himself. The VISTA trainer 'suggests' that I give him my shirt to wear. Great.

An hour or so later we're finally coming in for a landing in the village of Sleetmute, Alaska. With me in my undershirt. Great.

SLEETMUTE

Sleetmute!

The foothills of the Alaskan Range. The bank of the mighty Kuskoquim River. About twenty log cabins spread out along a dirt trail. Maybe a hundred Eskimos. Spruce and birch forests forever.

No television. No telephone. No electricity. No plumbing. No roads. No streets. No sidewalks. No cars. No signs. No business. No jobs. No law.

But there was a post office (zip code 99668), a one-room schoolhouse (Bureau of Indian Affairs) and two miles upriver and on the other bank, a trading post.

It was summer. It was warm. It was green. It was blue. It smelled good. It was primitive. It was magnificent.

After all the talk, training and travel, this was the end of the line and, as the VISTA plane took off and faded from sight, I could only wonder what would come next.

THE FIRST DAY

An hour or so after we arrived another plane landed on the grassy runway behind the village. It brought back the body of a fourteen-year-old village Eskimo girl who had died of tuberculosis.

It was very depressing. It seemed like a bad omen. I was young then and death was supposed to be remote. This was so close. A fourteen-year-old girl! And tuberculosis? I hadn't heard the word in years. It was a terrible way to start the year.

I felt very confused. This was too real, too soon. I knew I was sent to 'help' the Eskimos but, despite talk and training, I knew that I knew nothing. I couldn't help anybody. I came up with the idea that maybe if no one else dies this year then it would be a successful year. It was a childish and somewhat meaningless notion, but it was all I had at the time and it kept me going without having to think too much about it again.

I'VE GOT MAIL 2

Like I said, there's a post office. The wood sign above the door said SLEETMUTE POST OFFICE. It was hand carved.

I'm hoping maybe I've got a letter or somebody's sent me some pot. I open the door and walk in. I'm now in a dark room, the full width of the cabin and about three feet deep. Ah! A place for guns and parkas. Another wood door was right in front of me. I opened it and walked in.

I froze. I'm standing in somebody's house. It's one big room. A woman is washing a little kid in a metal tub on the floor. She doesn't acknowledge my presence. I remain frozen. She continues washing the kid. I continue to freeze. Finally Caswell comes in, and seeing the scene, figures out what's happening.

"He's Resnicoff", he said, pointing at me (still frozen). "He wants to know if he has any mail". Without saying anything she got up and went to a closet with Dutch doors, took out a key and opened up the post office; a closet with a rack of wooden pigeonholes on its back wall. She got some mail and handed it to me, still frozen.

"Let's go", said Caswell. And we did.

THE FIRST NIGHT

The village seemed deserted. We were told that a lot of the men had gone off to fight forest fires. We had been warned by VISTA not to mess around with the Eskimo women. They said it could only lead to trouble. It was the furthest thing from our minds that first night.

It's late. It's pitch black. We're both asleep when we're awakened by the door opening and we hear giggling. It sounds like giggling women, maybe three or four. It's too dark to see. They're creeping in, shushing each other, feeling their way around in the dark. They find Caswell in his sleeping bag. They're still giggling.

"Hey! Cut it out! What are you doing?" Caswell whimpered. Oh my God. They're tickling, groping and grabbing him. He's protesting but they're just giggling away. Maybe they were drunk. I don't know. Then they came looking for me.

I was terrified. I'm sure I stopped breathing and rolled myself up into a grapefruit-sized fetal ball. I remained absolutely motionless paralyzed by fear.

Somehow they didn't find me. Finally they left. It never happened again but at the time I was shaken.

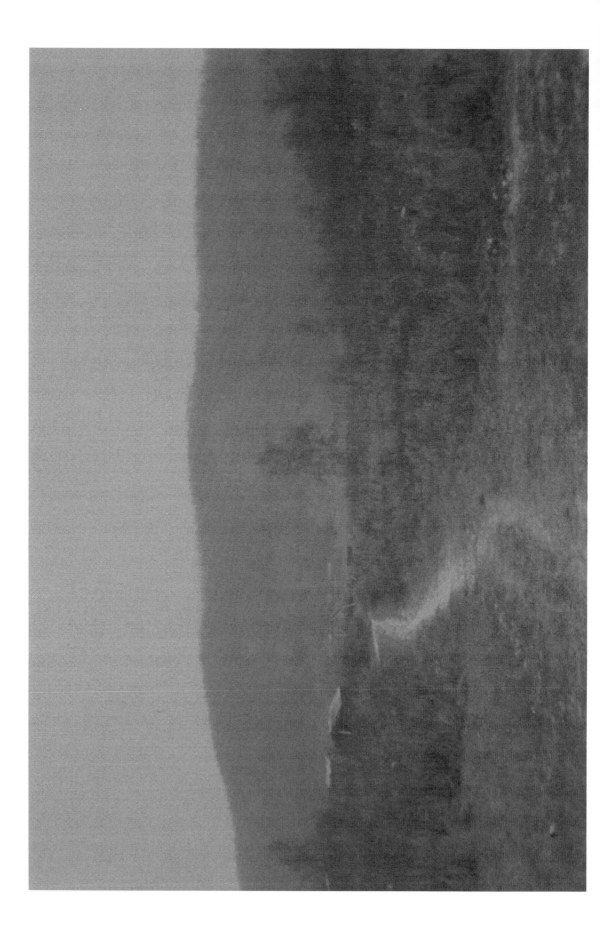

FAMILY

CULTURE SHOCK! I pretty much don't leave my room for several days. Caswell's out there learning who's who, learning the language and making friends. I'm making beans. I know I gotta go out sooner or later. Just as long as it's not now.

After four days or so I take a big breath and say to Caswell "Let's go for a little walk". It's late. I figure it's 'safe'. Caswell's been trying to get me out so he's ready. We take our flashlights and head down the dirt trail that winds through the center of the village. There are a lot of trees. There's noise and a campfire up ahead. It's a group of about 7 or 8 young Eskimo guys sitting around a blazing fire. They're drunk and they've seen us. This is not good.

One of them staggers over to Caswell. It looks like he's trying to focus on Caswell's face. "I'm Steve Abruska – who are you?" With the 'who are you' part of his question he pushes his finger hard into Caswell's chest. Oh shit, I'm thinking.

"I'm Phil Caswell". Abruska looks at Caswell from 3 or 4 different angles, still trying to focus. He uttered something in his very guttural Upic language. The others laugh.

Then he turned to me. "And who are you?" I got the finger in the chest too. "I'm Stan Resnicoff", I managed.

There was silence. All of a sudden the Eskimos are getting up and they seem to be dancing with me in a circle around the fire. Dancing! The party lasted for a little while. Soon I understood what they were saying. Turns out some of their names were Andrianoff,

Sergioff… Russian names…and I was Resnicoff! My name. My name linked me to these people.

Maybe Caswell and his little notepad were making friends, but somehow, from this drunken moment forward, I was family!

GUSSACH

Footnote: When the Russians owned Alaska, Sleetmute was the last village up the Kuskoquim River that they reached. Some died, some settled there and intermarried.The Eskimo word for white man is 'gussach', derived from the Russian 'Cossack'. It's not particularly complementary.

'Gussach'......and they can make it sound worse than it looks.

THE SWIM

One day soon after arrival I decided to go for a swim in the Kuskoquim River. It was still summer and warm. For some reason most of the Eskimos couldn't swim. Maybe this was something I could actually teach them.

The 'beach' was small and rocky. Lots of kids came to watch this. The water seemed very cold on my feet as I cautiously picked my way further out on the sharp rocks. When I was up to my knees I decided to bite the bullet and dive in.

EEEEEEYOOOOOWWWWWW! It's REALLY freezing and I'm already a half mile downstream. I had to fight, and I mean fight, my way out of the current. Then, near the shore I'm being rolled over the rocky bottom just trying to get a handhold. It wasn't pretty. By the time I could stand up again I was exhausted, cold, banged-up and way downstream.

It was a long, unpleasant barefoot walk back to the village. I learned that day why the Eskimos can't swim and I abandoned my Eskimo swim school plans.

KIDS

The kids were always around. They liked to watch me and my strange ways. They were also my best source of information.

I taught a little preschool class. I really didn't know what I was doing but that was certainly nothing new.

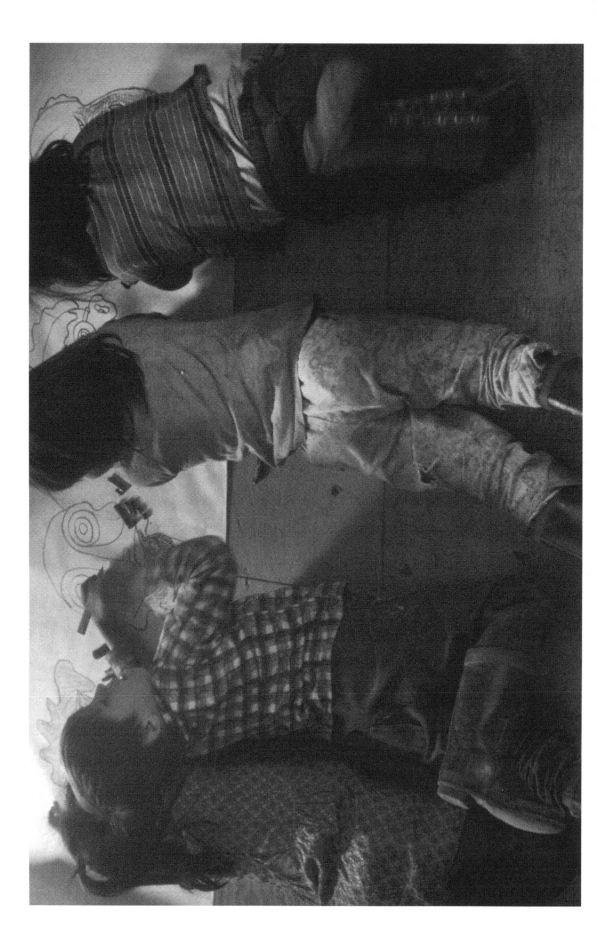

EXPECTATIONS

From the beginning there seemed to be a general misconception on the part of the Eskimos. I think they thought I had talents that could help them. They thought I knew what I was doing. They assumed I had the basic skills to survive. Why else would I have been sent?

There were times when I was doing something really stupid and they would sit and watch me thinking that I had discovered some new and better way.

They just didn't know how little I knew.

But they would soon figure it out.

DOGS & SNOWMOBILES 1

One day I happened to see this Eskimo guy walking quickly away, head down, and it looked like he was crying. Later I asked one of the kids and he told me why.

Another Eskimo guy in the village was planning to buy a snowmobile and didn't think he could afford to keep both his dogs and the snowmobile. The guy that I saw crying was 'hired' to shoot and bury the dogs.

THE NORTHERN LIGHTS

I had never seen the northern lights and really wanted to. I told the kids that if they were ever here to get me even if I was asleep.

So it's a couple of nights later and I'm asleep. They're knocking. "Stan, Stan, the lights! They're here!" I wake up and groggily walk to the door in my underwear. It's cold, I figure I'll take a quick look and jump back into the bed. I'm not expecting much. I opened the door.

My mouth dropped open. It was the most magnificent visual thing I had ever seen. Twin ruby red giant bands of light are traversing the black star-dotted night sky. Starting somewhere way behind me, they slowly undulated over my head and went all the way to some galactic horizon. It was moving sensually. It was alive. It was real.

I stood outside for an hour or so in my underwear, with my mouth still open. That good!

I saw the lights many more times. All different, all beautiful, but none as beautiful as that night.

ADVICE

After I had been in the village for a couple of weeks I took out my gun and went out for target practice. I was pitiful. I ran out of ammo before I ever hit any of the cans. One day an Eskimo guy who was shooting with me said casually, and NOT sarcastically, that if I ran into a bear, the best thing I could do with my gun would be to shoot myself in the head.

FISHING

In nature films the salmon are always seen jumping up falls. It's true but between the falls the salmon swim hundreds of miles upriver. I would have assumed they wouldn't swim right next to the shore but, of course, I was wrong. The river's current is strongest and fastest at its center and since the salmon are swimming against it, they cling to the shores. When the salmon are running there is an incredible carpet of salmon, fin to fin, head to head, fighting upriver right there! Inches away. For days. Incredible.

Different kinds of salmon run at different times, weeks apart. First I think it was the dog salmon, then the silver etc. I don't think I ever saw a rod and reel in the village. Fishing consisted of throwing a long straight net out into the river and almost immediately pulling it out. It would be packed with big salmon thrashing to be free. The combined weight of the salmon and the wet net made the nets heavy and hard to pull, and if not out soon they could become heavy enough so the current would pull the net out of the Eskimo's hands. The net and the salmon lost downstream.

Catching the fish you needed for the year didn't take long. Women spent days cleaning the fish and beautiful red salmon strips hung drying all over the village. Eskimo smoked salmon strips were, to me, the single greatest taste in the universe. And it was free.

B . I . A.

There was a school in the village. It was a Bureau of Indian Affairs School. Since the Eskimos weren't 'Indians' it was nominally insulting already but that's old news.

It was a one-room schoolhouse with quarters for the teacher. It had oil heat. It had a generator and electricity and a radio receiver-transmitter. It had white clapboards.

Late in the fall the teacher arrived. He was old. He had a real hearing problem. He didn't want to be here. He needed some more government teaching time or credits so he could retire. This was the only assignment left. The end of the line. He subscribed to his local Lubbock, Texas newspaper so that he could read the obituaries. He hardly ever left the schoolhouse. He was a nice man but the whole thing seemed sad.

I hardly ever went to the schoolhouse that year, even though I knew I could always be warm there. The B.I.A was the government and I wanted to be as much a part of the village reality as I could, but still, sometimes I wondered how different from that teacher I really was.

MY CHOICE

After a month or so in Sleetmute I get a message from VISTA to pack up all my stuff and catch the next mail plane into Anchorage. Nothing more. I thought that I was being fired and I couldn't imagine why. I hadn't done anything wrong. I hadn't done much of anything.

It took a couple of days to make the connections and when I finally got to the VISTA Anchorage office I found out, that far from being fired, VISTA had another assignment for me. Was it Hawaii? Surprisingly nobody there seemed to know anything more except that now I was supposed to head to the VISTA regional headquarters in San Francisco. OK.

More travel. Finally I'm at some big Federal building in San Francisco meeting with the regional head of VISTA. Everyone's real friendly as they tell me what this is all about. They heard that I was not too thrilled with Alaska and they were offering me an assignment here in San Francisco, in an area called the Tenderloin, which was a rather raunchy part of town. I was very surprised by this.

So let's see. It's the Tenderloin (San Francisco, drugs, prostitutes, porn etc.) vs. Sleetmute (Alaska, adventure, Eskimos, cold etc.).The truth was that it was no contest. After just a short time in Sleetmute, I too was starting to fall under the spell and majesty of Alaska. It took me all of two seconds to let VISTA know that if it was really up to me I definitely wanted to stay in Sleetmute. They seemed pleased and perhaps a bit surprised but soon I was unpacking my duffle bag again in Sleetmute. But this time it was my choice.

Two days later it started to snow.

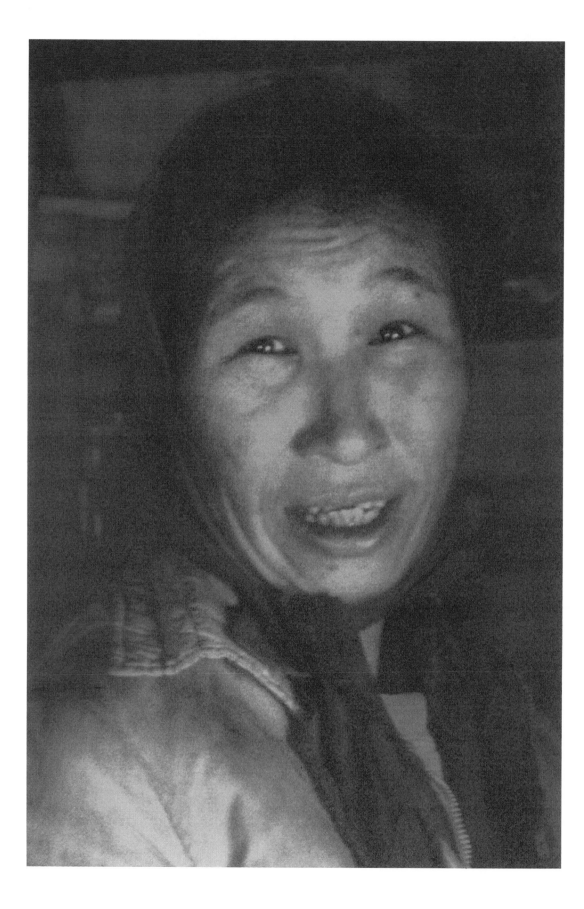

THE FIGHT

"COME! ...COME NOW...COME NOW!"

The hysterical Eskimo woman was pulling at me pleading for me to come with her. "THEY'RE GONNA KILL EACH OTHER."

I remembered VISTA's advice to steer clear of fights, but here I was, protesting, but being dragged along anyway. We got into her boat and were heading across the river to the one home on the other side. I'm not only headed towards a fight but I'm away from the village. Great. Where's Caswell when I need him? As we approach the bank I hear screaming and crashing coming from inside the cabin.

As I opened the door I see two guys, drunk to the gills, holding and punching each other with great success. They're both bloody and really banged up. Their drunkenness took the edge off the ferocity of the fight but it didn't lessen the damage. The place is trashed. They're still going at it and aren't even aware of me. What could I do? I yelled, as loud as I could "HEY, HOW CAN YOU TWO FIGHT WHEN YOU'RE BOTH MY FRIENDS! Well, either the loudness or the stupidity of my remark seemed to strike some nerve and they both stopped pummeling each other long enough to a) agree with me and b) offer me a drink. In the interest of continued peace I accepted. We sat. We drank a couple of beers. They looked terrible but they were feeling no pain.

Later on the ride back I felt pretty good that I had actually done something... somehow I'd stopped a fight.

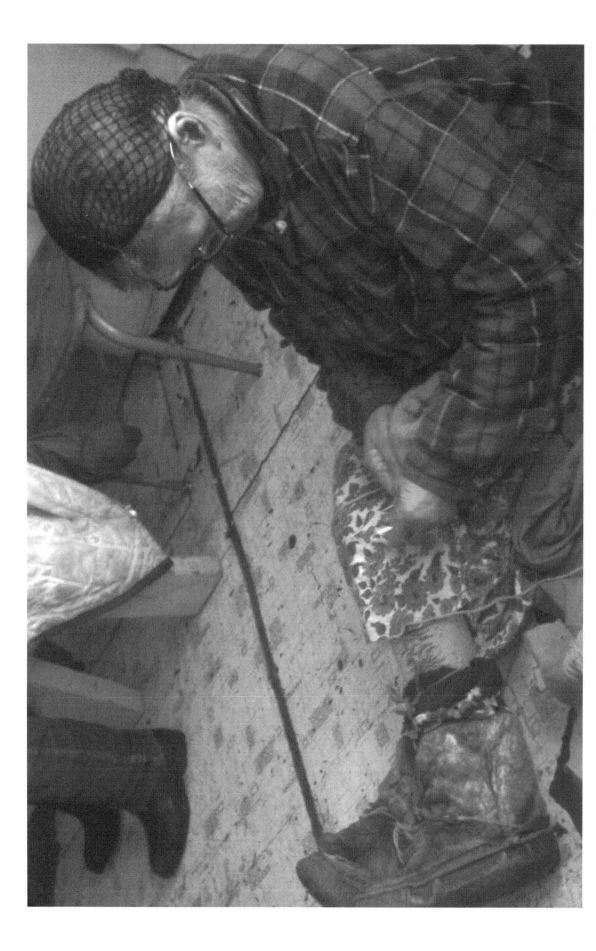

NON-VERBAL COMMUNICATION

The Eskimos were pretty non-verbal, and not just because I didn't speak Upic. They just didn't talk a lot. Not much chit chat. If they didn't have something to say, they didn't say it.

This was fine with me. As the year progressed I saw there could be conversations without talking and laughter without words.

THE TRADING POST

Two miles away, and on the other side of the river was the trading post. It was a real 'trading' post, taking in furs and giving credit for store-bought goods. The wooden shelves had canned vegetables, powdered milk etc. as well as ammo and cigarettes.

The post was run and owned by Nixie Mellick and his family. Nixie was a unique individual. His father was European and his mother an Eskimo. While he grew up in Sleetmute, totally integrated into every facet of native life, he also went and graduated from Bowling Green college in Ohio. He was smart in two worlds.

He was also a pilot with his own super cub plane.

Nixie knew Sleetmute and it's people in ways that I never would, and I got the feeling he also knew how little, if any, effect I would have on anything.

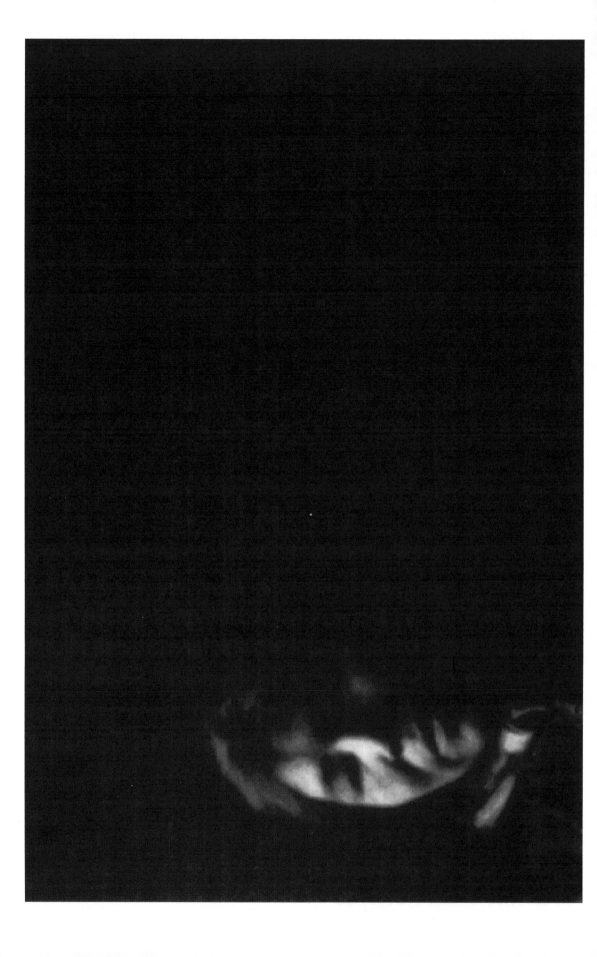

THE WORLD

One woman told me she couldn't read, write or tell time and she had never been more than thirty miles up or down the Kuskoquim River from Sleetmute.

SURVIVAL OF THE FITTEST

Stereotyping any group of people is more difficult as you get to know its individuals. As time went by I only saw the villagers of Sleetmute as individuals. Nonetheless, there was one common trait among the men. They were short and strong. Really strong. They were incredibly tough. They had small waists, broad shoulders and powerful legs. They were tireless. They were the perfect match for the brutality of their environment. They were the environment.

Now, what was I doing here again?

SNARES

The Eskimos caught rabbits with snares. I wondered what a snare was. It turns out that they're just wires that are made into little nooses. They're hung around the woods, and during the night the rabbits just seem to run, head first, into the nooses and die.

How was this possible? It's just a tiny little wire loop in a great big forest. It seemed to me that the rabbit would have to search for the snare and almost want to get caught.

It turns out the snare is placed along a rabbit trail. Trails were easy to see with any snow at all on the ground. Trails weren't rabbit 'highways' but the path of one rabbit from the previous night. The snares are placed between the footprints. The rabbit knows that it was safe on this trail last night and will often not only stay on it again but will actually run in the exact footprints that it had before.

Habit! A creature of habit!

I realized how like the rabbit I was. I wondered if you could see my footprints in New York if they would all be in the same places.

MY STOVE

I inherited some things in Sleetmute. One was my stove. It was two-thirds of an oil drum. It was cut along the first ridge, a round steel cover was hammered onto the top and a hole cut into it for the flue. There was a little metal door in front.

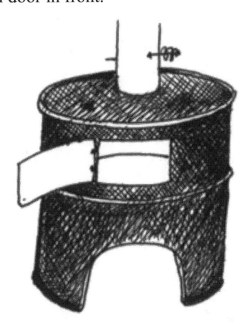

Sand was put into the bottom to keep it from burning through. The door kind of swung on little handmade hinges and fell off pretty much every time I touched it. The leftover piece of the drum held up the stove and provided a little wood storage underneath. The stove was small. It was inefficient and it ALWAYS went out well before morning. When I woke up the temperature inside was the same as the temperature outside. There was just a little less wind inside.

Nonetheless, I worshipped my stove. I spent, not hours, but months watching its flames dance inside. I treated it as if it was the only thing keeping me alive. Because it was.

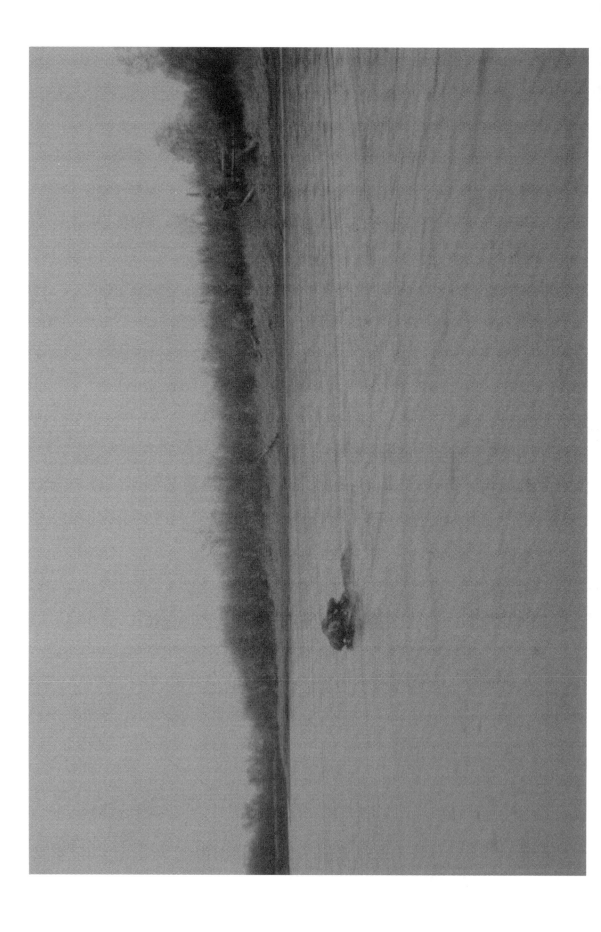

THE HUNT

Tomorrow Jack says he's taking us hunting. I'm not a hunter. I'm the kind that catches flies alive and sets 'em free outside rather than killing them. Still, I'm looking forward to the experience. I didn't think we'd catch anything anyway.

The next day we spent the entire morning and afternoon cutting wood for Jack. I'm thinking, "What a gyp!" Finally, about 5 in the afternoon, after we'd carried A LOT of wood, we're getting into a boat and heading upriver. I'm handed a 22 rifle, a relatively little gun. OK with me. It's already getting late and I'm sure this is gonna be just a boat ride.

The river was monotonously beautiful but after awhile, instead of keeping my eyes peeled on the banks for game, I started reading a paperback. At the time I thought it might be insulting and maybe not the right thing to do but I didn't really care. I was still a little pissed off about the whole wood carrying deal.

As we're rounding a bend I happen to peer up over the pages and I see something move behind a log. I point. They swing the boat around. Everybody's looking but there's nothing. We approach. There! Something moves again. Guns are raised but no shots are taken. It's gone, but they all saw it. "What?", I asked. "A wolverine", someone said without comment.

Whoa! Pure chance! Sheer luck! The gussach spots a wolverine. A wolverine! The smartest and 'stealthiest' animal around and I spotted it. While reading a book. Imagine if I paid attention. Anyway it felt good and we resumed upstream.

Fifteen minutes later. BOOM! BOOOM! BOOM! FUCK! My whole head's ringing as big guns explode right next to my ear. We're heading fast towards the shore. There's a small ball of fur writhing on the beach. The boat smashes ashore. The Eskimos rush up the hill into the brush. The fur ball is screaming! Crying! Oh God it's a baby bear!

There's a giant tree-crushing crunch and roar coming down the mountain straight towards the Eskimos. BOOM! BOOM! More trees collapsing towards me until a giant bear rolls out of the cover with enough momentum to carry it ten feet to the water's edge. Dead. The men yell at me to shoot the little bear. Its cries are almost human. I shot it, more than once until it stopped. This whole thing happened in twenty seconds. I was stunned. I was crying.

I don't remember the trip back to the village but when we got there it was dark and everyone was waiting for us on the beach. The bears were carried up to Jack's where there was a giant fire already burning outside. They were skinned, cut-up and roasted right there, with everyone in the village eating. It was a feast.

I was still confused by the whole thing but I also hadn't eaten all day and maybe hunger beats all other emotions because all I knew was that when I ate what I was handed, it tasted good. Very, very good. The hunt had been successful that day and the whole village ate. That night hunting stories were told around the fire. I thought I even heard something about me spotting the wolverine.

Finally I was so full and tired that I just fell asleep without having to think any more about anything.

It was a hell of a day.

DIET

That year I ate moose, bear, beaver, muskrat, spruce chicken, king, silver, red and dog salmon and grayling.

I passed on porcupine.

DINNER

The women cooked and served the food, usually some kind of stew. The men then ate. The women and children waited quietly until the men were finished. Whatever was left was theirs.

That was the way it was.

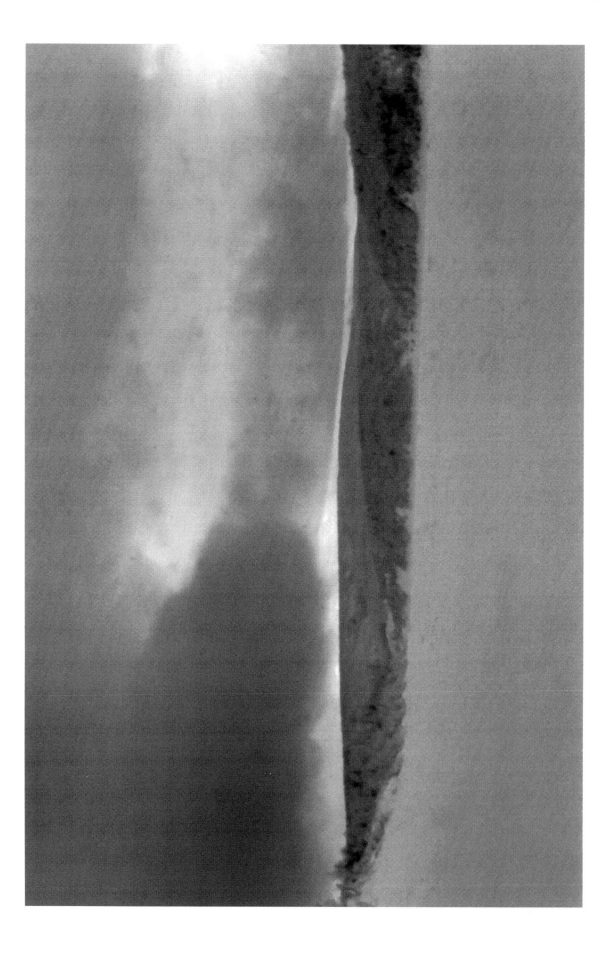

TIMING

The river begins to freeze from both banks towards the middle and by December it is frozen completely over. Before that happens though there's a time when there are large ice shelves on both banks and a big rushing river between them.

This was a tough time to cross the river to get to the trading post. The Eskimos would push a boat further and further to the edge of the ice shelf until the combined weight of the boat and the men caused the ice to crack off. At that exact moment everybody jumped in.

Now this might be natural if you've been doing it all your life but for me it was terrifying. You are far from the shore. You push and push knowing that any second the ice is gonna give and you gotta jump aboard. The river's loud. You can't jump in too soon or you're just a fool sitting in the boat with these other guys still pushing. Jump too late and you die.

Anyway, I survived.

THE HUNT 2

The next hunt was completely different. It was much colder now. For whatever reason we hiked for hours and hours over and through every kind of miserable terrain and brush.

I was freezing and falling behind (as usual) when I heard the shots up ahead. By the time I got there the men were standing around a huge dead moose. They began to skin it and cut it up. The only thing that I remember from cleaning and gutting the moose was how warm its body was. It was cut into five huge, still warm, pieces for each of us to carry. I couldn't believe how heavy the leg I was given was or how far I was going to have to carry it. My parka was soon covered with blood as I lugged on. Finally we made it back.

Hunting was very hard in a lot of ways, but I tried as best I could to do my part. I didn't know it at the time but my share of this hunt pretty much gave me enough meat to last until the salmon returned, and I didn't have to hunt again.

MY CACHE

My cache was a small shed. It was already below 32 degrees so whatever I stored there pretty quickly was frozen solid. Most every day during the winter I used a hacksaw to cut off a piece of moose for lunch or dinner.

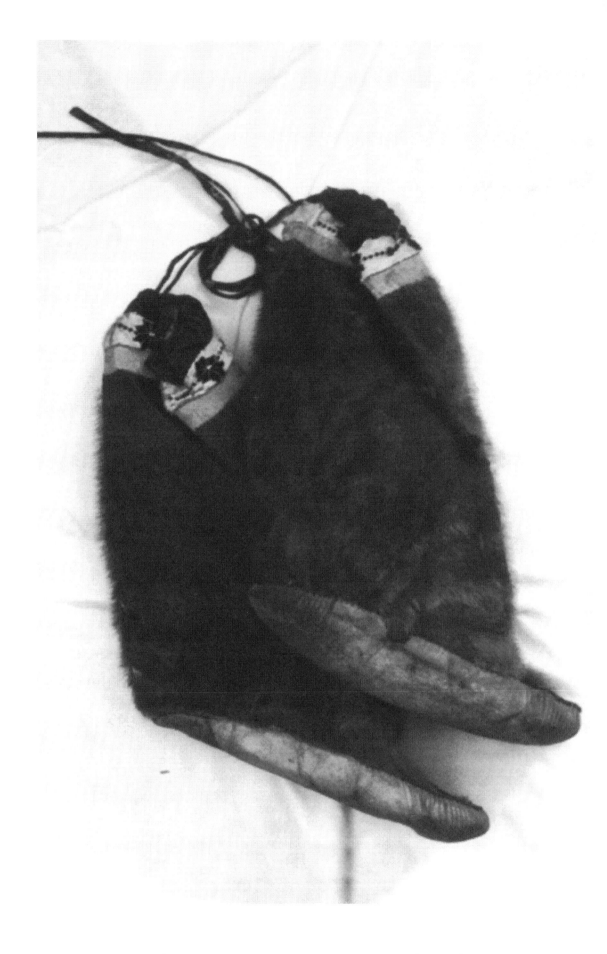

MUKLUKS

The Eskimo ladies in the village traced outlines of my feet onto paper and sent them to ladies they knew in some other village near the coast. Sometime later my sealskin mukluks arrived. They were beautiful. See?

They're no good when wet and useless on rocks and dirt, but on ice and snow, when the temperature dips to forty or fifty below NOTHING works like mukluks with a nice layer of dried grass inside.

My fingers froze, my hands froze, my ears froze, my ass froze and my eyeballs even froze once but my feet, my feet were always warm in those mukluks. Amazing.

DOGS AND SNOWMOBILES 2

For millennia (I guess) Eskimos had their dog teams and sleds. Now there are snowmobiles. Here's how they stack up.

	DOGS	**SNOWMOBILES**
COST	Negligible	Extraordinary (Biggest purchase after outboard motor)
FUEL	Fish, Gristle etc.	Gasoline
WEATHER	The colder it gets, the better the dogs like it. Always ready to go.	Never intended to function at 50 below. Sometimes ready to go.
INTELLIGENCE	Smart enough to get home by themselves and not to crash through thin ice.	None
NOISE	When pulling, the dogs are quiet. They don't scare away game	Extraordinary
RANGE	Think Ididerod	100 miles
SPEED	Slow	Fast
RELIABILITY	Yes	No
MAINTENANCE	Fish	Mechanical
CULTURAL INTEGRITY	Totally integrated into the Eskimo way of life.	Totally disruptive
STATUS	Old	New

Ahhhhhh. Progress.

ICE CREAM

The Eskimo women occasionally made 'ice cream' from fish. I think they whipped cooked salmon into a frothy consistency, added lots of sugar and froze it outside. It wasn't ice cream but it was wonderful.

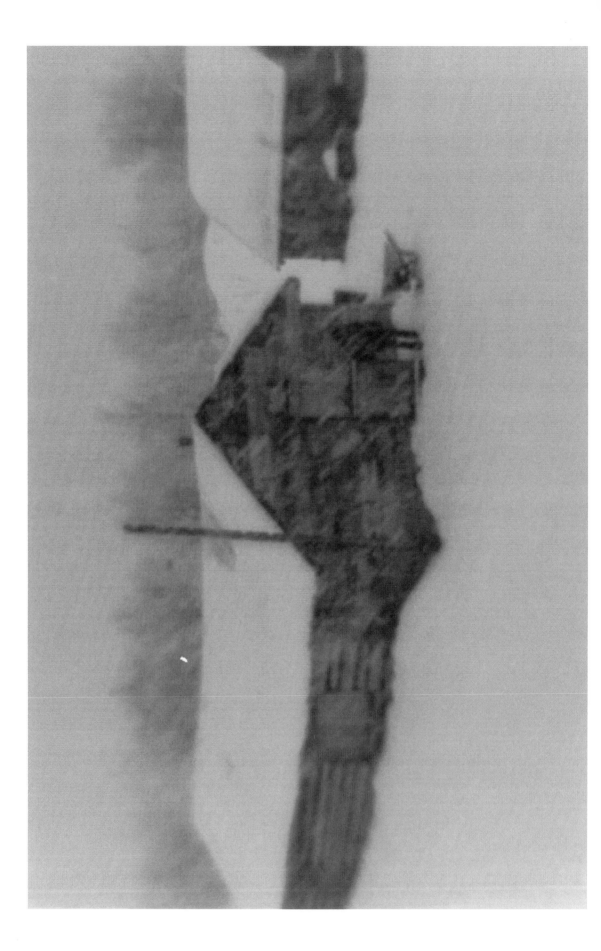

KNOCK – KNOCK

You didn't have to knock on someone's door to go in. You just went in. I think this comes from the fact that in the winter waiting outside would be just stupid and knocking would be ineffectual. I wasn't sure that this 'privilege' extended to me but I wanted it to so I just did it.

NICK FOGEY

Nick Fogey reminded me of my dad. His real last name was Andreanoff and I had no idea where the Fogey came from. He had a wife and four kids and a nice cabin near the end of the village. I felt comfortable visiting him. I talked more with him than with any of the other villagers. And when we had nothing to say, that was fine too. I remember his warm smile.

The village, like any other community had its range of providers. Some families always had meat put away while others depended upon catching a rabbit that night for dinner. Nick was a great provider. His table always had some delicacy from another season that tasted so good after months of moose.

During the whole year I visited Nick no more than a dozen times or so but they were warm times and I considered Nick to be my best friend in Sleetmute.

ANCHORAGE

After four months in the villages, VISTA flew all the volunteers back to Anchorage for a conference to see how we were all doing. We got on the next mail plane, flew downriver to Aniak where we caught a larger plane, a deHavilland Otter, that was capable of flying over the Alaska Range and into Anchorage. The Alaska range is the worlds second biggest, after the Himalayas .

Being in Anchorage was like being in a different world now and it was great to see everyone again and trade stories. I don't know about everyone else but just lying in a hot bath was worth the trip. VISTA was surprised to see my parka covered in blood, but to me it was normal.

The first thing that I did after the bath was to trade in my useless pistol for a 30-06 rifle. A big gun. No use fooling around anymore. The second thing I needed was one of those old iron crank meat grinders that I found at a pawn shop.

After my mukluks, my grinder was my most important acquisition. My winter diet was going to be moose. And more moose. My grinder empowered moose burgers. Much better.

After a couple of days we were headed back to Sleetmute....and the start of the real winter.

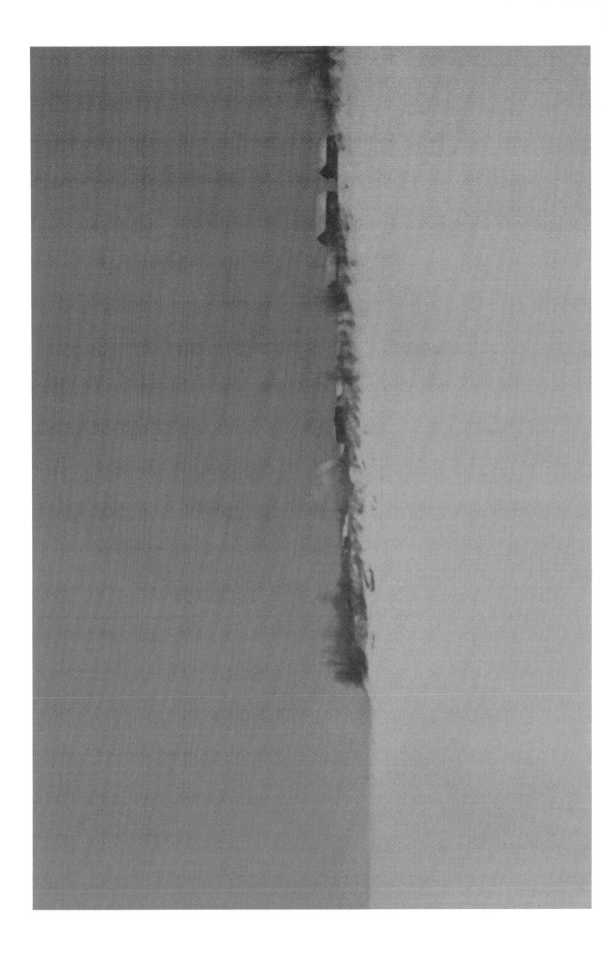

CHANGES

Fall was coming to an end and the weather was turning colder. The snow was falling and the days were getting shorter. There seemed to be a whole new rhythm of life starting.

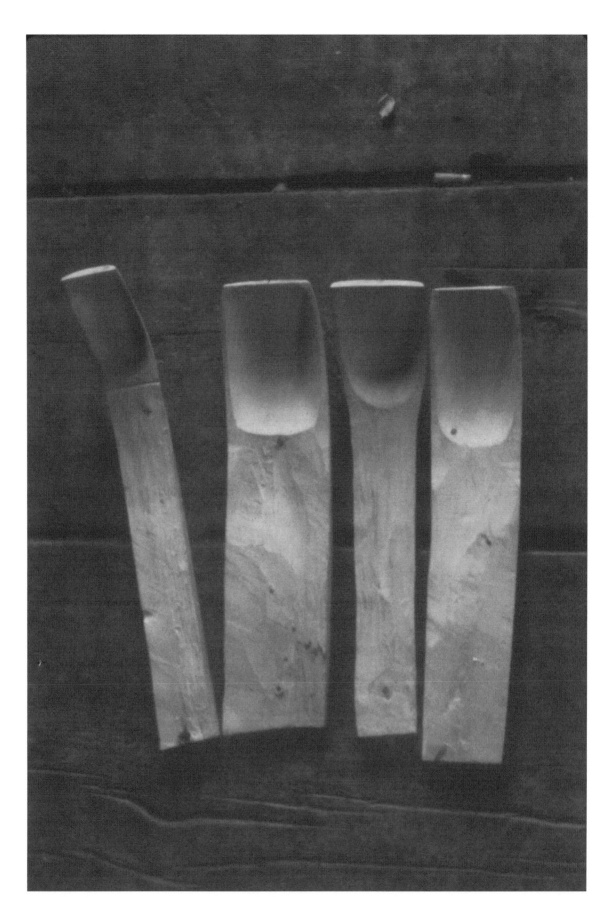

ANY MANY

Me: "How many more hours?"
Eskimo: "Any many"

Any many. The Eskimo term for anything more than two. A little more than two or a lot more. Same answer. Any many. It was applicable to any question.

Verbal communication had its limits and loveliness. The words, like the Eskimos themselves, were finely tuned.

BEST ON THE KUSKOQUIM

One cold night I'm in my sleeping bag just falling asleep when I hear my door open. It's an Eskimo girl and without any talking she's undressing and getting into my sleeping bag with me.

All the warnings I had been given about this disappeared with the touch of her warm body and when she whispered to me that she was "the best on the Kuskoquim", I was hers. She left before dawn.

The next day I was one happy volunteer but kinda scared. One of the things that's true about an Eskimo village is there are few secrets, everybody knows your business. When I wasn't shot over the next couple of days I figured everything was cool with the villagers and I had reached another level of acceptance.

When she could, she would sneak over, and the winter, as brutal as it was, was sweeter and not as cold because of her.

ITULILIK

Two Eskimo guys invited me to come to their trapping camp, Itulilik, for a winter visit. For some Eskimos, Sleetmute was as busy as Times Square. They needed space.

I was flattered to be invited but I kept putting off going because I didn't know what I was getting myself into. I also noticed that great pain seemed to be associated with my leaving the village for any reason. But curiosity got the better of me and one day I hitched a ride on the mail plane to Itulilik, about twenty minutes away.

Itulilik looked like an abandoned village. There were three or four abandoned cabins. Some had collapsed. The guys were happy to see me but I had missed their trapping season (thank God) so I couldn't go trudging all over the wilderness with them. We really didn't do much the week I was there. They had cooked up a batch of home brew, which couldn't possibly taste as bad as it looked, but it did.

Caswell wasn't invited on this trip but I was friendlier with these guys anyway.

One thing they did have was a steam bath. It was a little log cabin, like a big doghouse. It was maybe three feet on each side, and also three feet tall. There was a small door in front. A steam bath sounded great and I was really looking forward to it. I had heard that the Eskimos used the steam bath as a test of manhood and they would try to see who could withstand the hottest steam. But it was probably twenty below now and no amount of heat sounded bad to me.

We got in and took our places around an already pretty hot fire with glowing rocks. I was against the back wall, directly opposite the door, with the other guys on either side of me.

We each took turns passing a ladle and pouring water on the rocks. The resulting steam was initially brutal and quickly became frightening. We had bunches of twigs that we could push against our faces to theoretically cool the scalding air before it entered our lungs, but they were irrelevant. With each pour the temperature elevated to the point where I was sure that I was going to pass out, fall into the fire and die, not necessarily in that order.

They, of course, were having a ball. I thought about making a break for the door, but the only path was directly over the fire, and the roof was real low.

Finally, I was sure that even falling into the fire would be cooler than the air I was baking in and I made my move. I dove over the fire and through the small door, landing naked in the snow outside. Alive! Alive! I danced around. I was alive and it felt great.

That was my last steam bath.

I found out later that VISTA thought it was a big deal for me to have been to be invited to Itulilik. I guess.

THE 'FRIENDLY' VISTA

I returned to Sleetmute from Itulilik. I was glad to get home. The first thing someone says to me is something like "tell Caswell peoples didn't mean it". "What?", I asked. Nobody said much. I found Caswell. He told me what happened.

Thanksgiving was two days ago. Caswell had gone to Olinka's house because there was some kind of party. Unfortunately there was drinking. Now I might have mentioned that Caswell was referred to as 'the friendly VISTA' (the implication was obvious). He did things with the people, he cut wood for people, he was learning the language and writing down who was related to whom. He packed water for Olinka.

Everybody liked Caswell. As he told it, sometime during the party one of the drunken men told Caswell it was OK with everyone if he married Olinka. (Olinka's husband had died going through the ice a couple of years before). This of course was a complete surprise to Caswell and when he told them that he didn't want to marry anyone, people were offended and in the ensuing liquor-fueled brawl two of Caswell's ribs were broken. A 30-06 was also shot off inside the cabin. The whole thing could have been much worse.

Seems the Eskimos had all interpreted Caswell's willingness to help and his friendliness as courting. Alcohol did the rest.

The next day everyone was apologetic and embarrassed. But Caswell was hurt. It wasn't just his ribs. He felt everything he had tried to do had come to nothing. He told me he was leaving. We talked but his mind was made up. Later that night, as he packed, I confessed that I had had an Eskimo girlfriend for the last month or so. This was the last straw for Caswell.

The friendly VISTA left on the next morning's mail plane.

It was November. I was alone.

I have to admit, I liked it better.

FOOD STAMPS

The government had given us a pamphlet about the Eskimos. It was titled 'The Poorest Americans'. They lived a non-cash subsistence life and they lived off the land. Their customs, habits, rituals and daily life were perfectly in tune with their environment. But this was 1969, and they were Americans in the era of Lyndon Johnson's Great Society. The Eskimos were entitled to food stamps.

They would check off forms and weeks or months later cases of the strangest food arrived by mail plane. I had mixed feelings about the whole thing. I saw that the hunting ritual passed more from father to son than just hunting skills. It was a survival ballet. It was timeless teaching tool about their world. And here comes the government with cases of Vienna sausage. It reminded me of the American Indian stories I had heard.

We talked about it but the Eskimos also knew that I was on the Government's payroll. I got my 'fix' from the government, why shouldn't they? They didn't say it in the same words but the message came across. Besides if I was there to help, at least sometimes it had to be on their terms.

I never liked Vienna sausages much since then.

MUSH

My efforts to drive a dog team were 'semi-successful'. Once I had to leave the village and go through the woods to pick us some firewood. This is not open space like the river. It's heavily wooded with trails and muscling the sled around behind the dogs is hard work. It's debatable whether I was driving the dogs or they were driving me. Anyway I made it, loaded the sled with the firewood and set out for home.

The sled was a lot heavier now. The dogs strained to get it moving. The hard part of driving is when the dogs go around a tight curve you have to push the sled straight ahead on the trail so it doesn't 'cut the corner' and get pulled into the trees. Tell me about it. On the second switchback I'm in the trees. The sled crashes and overturns. The firewood all falls out and the dogs, with their new lightened load (no firewood, no me) dash on towards the village with the empty sled, on its side, crashing around behind them. I'm sitting on my ass in the snow watching them disappear.

A couple of hours later I walked back into the village. Nobody was around but they all knew. I thought that I even heard the dogs laughing somewhere.

EXPLODING WOOD

Wood was warmth. Wood was life. Burning wood was easy. Splitting wood was hard.

One day when it was very cold, I heard a new sound coming from all over the village. A sound I realized I hadn't heard in months. All of a sudden everybody was splitting wood. Turns out the Eskimos wait until the temperature drops to just the right point, maybe 35 below, before they split wood. At that temperature the moisture content in the wood freezes solid and splitting wood becomes just like cracking ice. Easier.

I tried it. The wood seemed to just blow apart. Wow. It was actually fun.

Exploding wood!

THE TIN MAN

It was probably January when I decided to move a short distance into an abandoned log cabin right on the riverbank. Now there were two things I didn't know. First, it was abandoned because it's too cold right on the river, and if that wasn't enough, this cabin had been lifted up in a flood and rotated so now its front door faced north. Right into the wind. I didn't know. I thought it looked good. It was impossible to heat.

That night, with no warning, I got sick. Really sick. I became very weak. I had a fever and I was burning up. I felt terrible and to top it off I had to take a wicked shit.

I can't claim to have been thinking clearly but the only thing on my mind was to make it to the little outhouse near my previous cabin. It wasn't far. Maybe 2 football fields away. I already had on two pairs of thermal woven cotton long-johns. I put on sweaters. I got on my parka. I opened the door.

It was brutal. Maybe 40 below. It was 4 am. The moon lit the snow. It was very quiet. I shuffled ahead, the only thought on my mind was the relief that was waiting for me inside the outhouse. My steps got shorter. I was holding it in. Occasionally I had to stop. The outhouse was only fifty feet away. I thought I could make it. I was wrong.

I lost control. Diarrhea, hot diarrhea blasted from me completely soaking the fabric of my long-johns, enveloping me momentarily in comforting warmth – and then – one second later –everything froze solid.

So now I'm sick, it's 40 below, I just shit in my pants and I'm immobilized with my legs encased in frozen excrement encrusted long-johns. I couldn't move.

I was the tin man. I quietly started to sob. And then I fell, face first, stiff as a board into the snow. I'm laughing as I write this. I wasn't laughing then.

I crawled into the empty community center building. I remember it took me a long time to somehow open the door. I crawled behind a cold stove. I got into the fetal position. I fell asleep. I remember hearing kids find me in the morning. I remember them calling their moms.

The next thing I remember is being poked. I'm waking up. It's dark. I'm in my bed. I'm naked. I'm clean. Something is hurting me. There's laughing. I open my eyes to see three Eskimo women poking me with willow brush branches. They're actually prodding me with branches and laughing at me. I was delirious. I remember trying to sweep them away with my arm. "Get the fuck away from me!" They kept laughing and poking. It was like a nightmare, laughing witch-like women torturing me all illuminated by the flickering fire. Mercifully everything finally went black.

The next day I was better. The fever had broken. I was very tired and weak. I remembered the outhouse, and the tin man and the women and the branches. They all seemed very far away. What seemed like one night to me then may have been more. I think those women saved my life.

We never talked about that night.

NIGHT HOWL

Night. Winter. The temperature is fifty-five below zero. The winds are blowing hard. The dogs are out there. Howling.

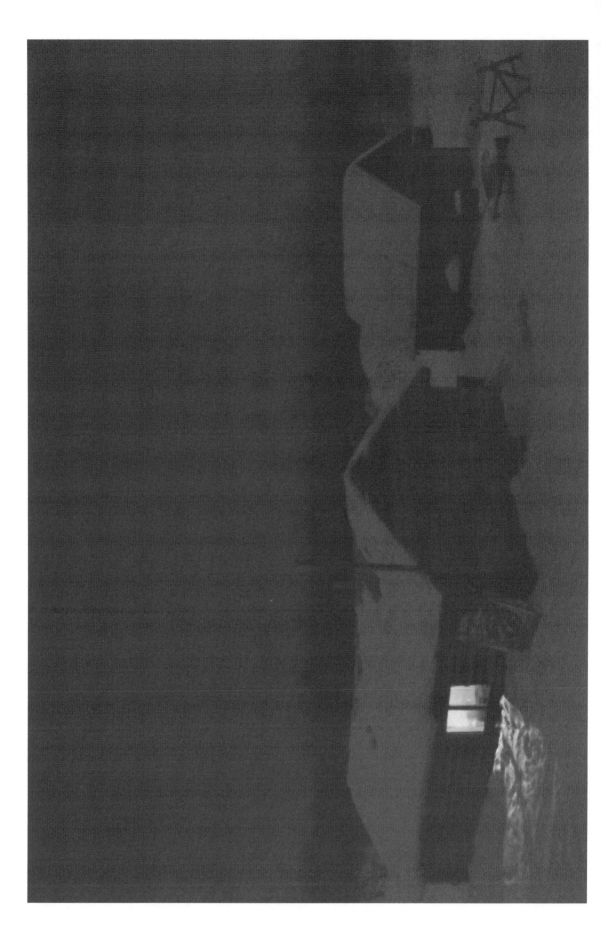

54 BELOW

The Eskimos had been here countless millennia but this was my first winter. Nobody can prepare you. You've got to feel it. Each ten-degree dip brings its own pain level. First it's thirty below for three weeks, then forty below for 2 weeks and then it goes down to minus fifty. And it's dark. The sun barely rises above the horizon, moves over an inch and then sets. Whoa. This was planetary.

The coldest I was in was fifty-four below. At fifty-four below the moisture on your eyeballs freezes. It's brutal. I wore every piece of clothing I owned. Life slowed to a crawl.

But then, in a week or so, the temperatures slowly rises, up to forty below, and guess what, it feels warm. Isn't relativity beautiful? After the winter I remember being outside completely comfortable in a T-shirt at twenty below.

After I felt the flow of the seasons I understood much more. But the first time through was a bitch.

MY FAVORITE
SNOWMOBILE STORY

Matvie was trying to start an old snowmobile. It was very cold. He must have pulled the starter cord a hundred times. The spark plug was loose and needed a gasket. There were no gaskets. Next I see he's cutting a gasket out of a leaf. I don't expect much but it works. On the next pull the engine catches and Matvie's off with a big smile on his face.

Later that afternoon I saw him and he's wearing this strange contraption. Somehow the spark plug hole threads were now completely stripped and in order to hold the plug in he had wrapped bailing wire around the belly of the snowmobile and around the top of the spark plug a couple of times. This worked, for a while, until all the wires rattled themselves loose and the spark plug shot into the air like a bullet. After he had just missed being killed by a flying spark plug he took a square piece of plywood and strapped it to his chest with more bailing wire. It kind of looked like the numbers on the chests of Olympic skiers.

So now he could use the snowmobile until the wires jiggled loose. The plug would then shoot out, hit him in the plywood plate on his chest and blow him backward off the snowmobile, which was stopping anyway. He would pick himself up, reattach the wires and he was off again.

I might not have believed it but one look at the burnt and scarred plywood on his chest was convincing. It was Matvie's system, and it worked.

HANDS

I came back from somewhere or something and my hands were totally without feeling. They were frozen. I was scared.

Was this frostbite? Have I actually done permanent damage? To my hands? You're trained to put your hands in your armpits or between your legs to *slowly* 'thaw them out'. I remember occasionally gently tapping my hand against the wall to see if I felt anything. Gently because I didn't want my hand to crack off.

After twenty minutes, which seemed longer, some, then all feeling returned. I was OK.

I swore that I'd never let that happen again.

Before the winter ended it happened once again.

RADIO

I had a small radio that picked up AM, FM and Shortwave stations. To pick up any signal at all I had to string up a 100 foot long wire antenna, and even then it was rare to receive anything. Batteries were also a bit hard to come by.

And then, late one night, as I slowly turned the dial thru endless static, I heard something. It just faded in so I didn't know what I was listening to. It seemed like religious music, a choir, but then, as the words and music and message built up to its crescendo I sat there straining to hear 'You Can't Always Get What You Want" for the first time. It faded out and was gone way before it ended.

You can't always get what you want?

Religious music?

Amen.

THIN ICE

The winter dragged on. One day Nattie told me that she heard that Nixie was going to get in touch with VISTA to 'come and pick up your volunteer because he isn't doing anything'. This wasn't good. No.

The next morning I bundled up and set out on a long lonely walk up the riverbank and then across the frozen Kuskoquim to the trading post. If it was cold I hardly noticed. Like I said earlier, Nixie understood Sleetmute in ways that I never could. I didn't know what I was gonna say. It was a long walk in more ways than one.

When I got to the trading post I asked Nixie if he had a couple of minutes to talk. He did. I told him what I had heard. He nodded. I told him that I agreed with him. He seemed surprised. I told him I didn't mean that I wanted to leave Sleetmute, I didn't, but I honestly wasn't sure what I could actually do.

I gave him this example. There were VISTA volunteers there before me. One project they had started was to bring electricity from the school to the community center. They organized the villagers to cut trees, made poles and placed them in the ground in a straight row between the two buildings. Then their year was up, they left, and the work stopped. It sure wasn't because the Eskimo people didn't know how to finish the job - they somehow knew more than I'll ever know. No. It seemed to me that the reason they did the project was more for the VISTAS than because they wanted it done or cared whether the community center had electricity or not.

To my great surprise Nixie laughed, and actually agreed with me. He understood what I was saying. He told me he knew I had a nice relationship with the people of Sleetmute. We talked about this or that. I asked for his help; what could I do that might matter. After a long talk we agreed that I'd re-start my little pre-school classes that I had abandoned after I got sick. Believe me, I wasn't much better at teaching kids than electrifying the village, but it would be something and Nixie seemed pleased. And I did too. We had tea.

The walk back to the village seemed much shorter. I heard later that Nixie gave me a lot of credit for facing up to the problem. But I didn't deserve any credit. It was just the truth.

And later that year Nixie would do me a big favor, one that I'll never forget or be able to repay, and for that too I would always be appreciative.

ARCTIC MISSIONS INC.

Three or four times a year the Arctic Missions Inc. piper cub flew into Sleetmute. Two missionaries, a husband pilot and his wife preached and held a Sunday school kind of meeting.

Most of the adults were Russian Orthodox and were polite but didn't participate much. The kids flocked to them. They gave out religious pictures to the kids, which were actually Christmas cards with the message cut off.

Although I probably needed all the spiritual help I could get, I didn't have much to do with them, and they never stayed more than a couple of hours.

Any arrival in the village was a big event.

LOST IN ALASKA

I don't remember where we were going or why.

We walked all morning. The ground was covered with fresh snow. I was getting tired. The Eskimos never got tired. I started to fall behind. It didn't matter because they left clear footprints in the snow that I could easily follow.

More walking. I couldn't see them or hear them any more. I just kept following the tracks.

Then it started to snow. The snow was filling in their tracks making them harder and harder to see. I stepped up my pace. The tracks got fainter. Finally I couldn't see them at all.

I did exactly what you're not supposed to do. I ran. Aimlessly. First in one direction, then another, then back until I was completely out of breath, exhausted. As I struggled to breathe the only thought that I could muster was the title of that old Abbot and Costello film "Lost in Alaska."

I was lost in Alaska.

I have no idea how but many hours later I walked back into the village. I think it was just luck. I was too tired to be relieved. I fell asleep.

I never admitted I was lost.

I'VE REALLY GOT MAIL!

Mail! A package from my parents. Everyone who was at the mail call followed me home to see what was in it. "Jew-Food!" Kosher salamis, pickles, gefilte fish, horseradish, halavah and other assorted cans and jars. Even canned salmon.

Just as the Eskimos had shared their moose and bear with me, I now could share with them. All of them.

They loved it! They ate everything! Each item was inspected, smelled, discussed (in Upic), tasted, devoured and discussed again. Everything was gone in a half-hour. What a joy! What a joy!

"SEE-YA LATER"

Grandma Charlie spoke almost no English. We got along very well together. I guess I would just visit and sit quietly for hours. She would always have tea.

This is the only picture I took of her. I gestured to the camera for permission. She nodded. It took me a long time to find just the shot I wanted. She held still. An instant after I snapped the shutter we both burst out laughing. It was perfect.

On another occasion I found out that she had stayed up most of the night waiting for me to return because when I had left earlier I had said " see-ya later."

I spoke more carefully, and even less, after that.

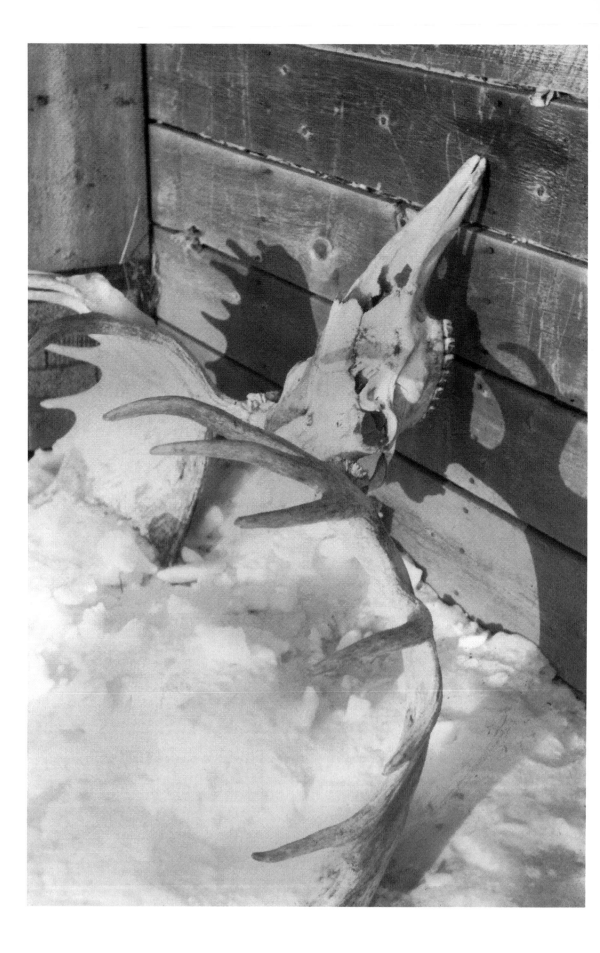

THE LEDGE

The Eskimos never hunted for sport. They hunted to eat; for subsistence. Nonetheless they were subject to the State hunting laws. They said the Game Wardens occasionally fly over and if they're caught hunting out-of-season they were in big trouble.

It was late March. Many families in the village had run out of meat. Some men had illegally killed a moose an hour or so away from the village and hid and camouflaged it because they didn't want to transport it in daylight. After dark, two snowmobiles set out to retrieve the moose. Jack, a cautious and competent Eskimo drove the first and for some reason I drove the second. We crossed the frozen river and went up a stream valley at speed. It was dark and only the snowmobile's headlight lit our path. We were going faster than I felt comfortable going but I was determined not to fall behind or, God forbid, get lost again. I stayed close behind. The valley narrowed and the walls got steeper and soon we were zipping along a narrow ledge, not much wider than the snowmobile's track and we're 30 feet above the valley floor. The trail twisted and turned. Jack didn't slow down and I stayed right on his ass. He was the Eskimo. He knew where we are going and why we're on that ledge and why the hell we have to be going so fast.

Then, without warning, Jack peels off the ledge, racing furiously down the steep slope and into the valley. I'm right behind. Maybe the trail was out ahead. We zip along the frozen stream bed for a little while and then Jack guns his snowmobile up the slope, having enough momentum to JUST make it back to the ledge. My heart's in my mouth as I climbed behind him, barely thinking of not making it up to the trail and falling backwards, snowmobile and all into the valley. I made it.

We sped along the ledge for another ten minutes or so and then Wham! Jack's banking into the valley again and we repeat the whole harrowing sequence. Finally we're back on the ledge. I'm covered with sweat. Jack stops his snowmobile. He gets off and walks back. He looks at me strangely and says, "When I fall off the trail you don't have to follow me."

THE VISIT

Falling through the river ice meant death. The ice-cold water quickly swept you away from the hole you'd fallen through. You drowned. In the spring somebody always found your body downstream. Your knuckles are bloody or broken from punching the ice in a futile attempt to free yourself.

After nine months my area supervisor, Jim Holton, was coming to visit and CHECK-UP on me. It was my worst nightmare come true. He would see that I had done nothing. I was doomed.

The day arrived. He would be landing across the frozen river at the trading post. I had to borrow a snowmobile to pick him up. He would be staying for only one day. I was still doomed.

Now, I have to explain the river ice at this time of year. It was still basically twelve feet thick, but during the day the temperature would get above freezing and some surface ice would melt. At night it would re-freeze, leaving a layer of still water between the thin surface ice and the big solid ice below. Thin ice – water – solid ice. I knew it, the Eskimos knew it, Jim didn't know it. As I crossed the river to get him I heard ominous cracks behind the snowmobile but I made it. I found Jim, and he climbed on behind me with his backpack. We were much heavier now.

I knew we had one chance to make it across – speed. The dozen or so Eskimos hanging around the trading post came out to watch. They knew.

I was ready. Any fear I had vanished. I let out a cowboy scream, gunned the engine to the max, sped straight down the steep bank and shot across the river ice like a bullet. Jim held on for dear life. I drove fast, picking my path carefully and whooping and hollering like a madman. Halfway across the ice starts to crack behind us. Jim screams at me. I laugh and try to go faster.

We're actually leaving a trail of broken ice and water behind us. I felt Jim's fingers claw into my parka. Twice we're slowed and start to tilt and sink backwards, only to have the track catch and shoot us up and forward again, spraying a rooster-tail of water behind us.

We almost made it. Near the bank I ran out of speed and luck at the same time and the snowmobile crashed through the ice. Jim's screaming. The engine floods and stalls and we're left standing in three feet of crushed ice and cold water. Way back across the river you could still hear the Eskimos laughing.

We walked a mile or so back to my place wet, cold and in silence. Even though I was still doomed, Jim seemed to be happy. He was probably happy just to be alive.

The next day the weather turned very bad. No planes. Jim would be with me for a week. If he was gonna see how little I'd done in a one day visit, imagine how much he'd see I hadn't done in a whole week. Doomed! Doomed! Doomed!

With the weather this bad there was little we could do except visit. I think we visited everyone in the village that week. We sat. We had tea. We 'talked story'. We ate. We sat more. I don't remember much more.

Finally the weather broke and Jim was going home. He was very happy which I was sure had more to do with his getting out of Sleetmute than with my performance as a VISTA volunteer. His plane's skis lifted off the ice and he was gone.

He was on his way to headquarters. I had been happy to have a visitor but still worried. He would write a report. I was doomed.

THOUGHTS OF HOME

Three weeks or so after Jim left the first taste of spring began to appear through the grays of winter. My thoughts turned to home. I got this idea. Maybe I could leave the village, get home to New York for a brief visit and back, without VISTA ever finding out. After all, except for Jim's visit and a couple of conferences, VISTA really didn't know if I was dead or alive. It was risky (and stupid) but I was probably doomed anyway with Jim's report.

I had the money. My VISTA checks (160 dollars a month) had been piling up under my bed. Not much to buy.

I told Nattie, the postmistress, and the others of my plan. I saw they didn't believe that I would ever come back but they sure understood the universal desire to go home. They said that if for some reason VISTA tried to contact me over the short wave they would say that I was out of the village camping or at fish camp or something. They would cover for me.

Now I just had to get to Anchorage. I couldn't take the mail plane because then everyone up and down the river would know my business, including VISTA. I told Nixie at the trading post what I was planning. He was also a pilot and had a Piper Super Cub that he was planning to take to Anchorage for regular service. He said I could hitch a ride.

We would be leaving tomorrow morning.

TAKE OFF

We're going to be flying through the Alaska Range, the second largest mountain range in the world after the Himalayas. Every other time I went to Anchorage I took the mail plane down river to a bigger landing strip where I could get a bigger plane that flew over the mountains. This time it wouldn't be 'over', it would be 'through'.

The mountains are huge. The super cub is small. A single engine, two seats, one behind the other. Very small.

Since we were going to be landing at Anchorage International Airport's concrete runway we had to take off with wheels, not skis. But we had to take off from the river ice and wheels weren't particularly designed for ice. Besides the traction issue, the wheels concentrated the weight of the plane in a much smaller footprint than the skis.

We got in. It was tight. We began to taxi when one of the wheels crashes through the ice into the water. We're spun around. The plane's right wingtip hits the ice, holding the plane up. Nixie kills the engine. We carefully and lightly get out. Nixie inspects the plane and doesn't see any structural damage. Next we go into the woods and chop down some small birch trees and drag them to the plane. We criss-cross them on the ice around the plane and then, standing on the branches to distribute our weight, gently lift the wing with our backs. When the wheel is free we roll the plane forward ten feet or so. There's another inspection and we get back in.

We start to taxi again and after what seems to me to be a long time, the wheels finally lift off the ice and we are climbing and headed toward some very big mountains.

THE ALASKA RANGE

An hour later we were in the mountains. They were over 20,000 feet tall. We flew at 4,000 feet. We wound our way, twisting and turning through the passes with rock and ice at times seemingly touching both wingtips. We flew through chasms and past active volcanoes. The scale was enormous and we were the tiniest single-engine gnat. Five hours. It was magnificent. At times my heart was in my mouth but I loved it.

There are usually two completely different weather systems on each side of the range. They meet somewhere near the middle of the pass. It's called 'the wall'. It looks like nothing until it just flips a plane into the rock. Or it can just be nothing. There was no wall for us that day but Nixie told me that if it were summer and if I could see the ground, I would see the remnants of crashed planes all the way through the pass.

Finally the big mountains changed into regular mountains, then into hills, then into mudflats and after we crossed Cook Inlet the wheels touched down on the tarmac at Anchorage International. I thanked Nixie for the ride of my life and I'm off to find a flight to New York.

NYC

Maybe someone could adjust to the Sleetmute/ New York juxtaposition, but not me.

After ten months in Sleetmute, the city was simply beyond my comprehension. I walked around like a tourist from some primitive world marveling at simple things like bricks, and curbs and signs. I touched everything and smiled at their beauty. I swooned at the implied cooperation it must have taken to build all this. My friends thought that I was seriously brain damaged.

I drove. It was a world of moving lights, shapes and colors. At 43rd and Broadway somehow I smashed my car into the side of a taxicab. The taxi driver jumped out pointing and screaming and blaming. I got out laughing. Laughing at the humor of the whole thing; a yelling man, horns blowing and cars driving all around us. In color. It was all too fantastic to be taken seriously. When the cab driver saw me laughing like this he stopped yelling, jumped back into his cab and just drove away. He looked scared.

But I wasn't really fitting in anywhere. This trip to New York was a mistake and at the end of a week or two I kind of eagerly got back on a Northwest jet for the start of the long trip back to Sleetmute.

BREAKUP

One day in May the frozen ice of the Kuskoquim River begins to breakup. Over 150 miles of still thick ice starts to fracture and then, all together start to move towards the coast and the Bering Sea. Giants chunks and sheets of jagged ice scrape and jostle each other as they jockey for position in the semi-frozen slush. The ice tears at the riverbank, ripping trees out of the earth and carving away the shoreline. It's big. It's powerful. It's primal and it's loud.

Some years the ice can get stuck rounding a bend creating a giant ice dam. The water and ice behind it rise. Whole villages can easily be swept away in these floods. But there were no ice jams this year.

Breakup was an incredible sight to see.

Unfortunately, I didn't see any of it because I was in New York.

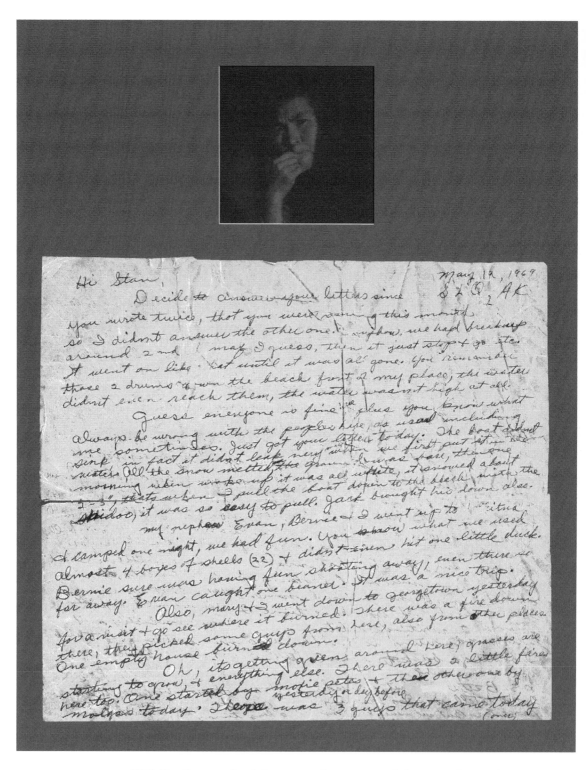

While I was in New York I stayed in touch with Sleetmute. Here is the letter Nattie wrote back to me.

The 'Mary' she refers to is Mary Mellick, Nixie's wife who ran the Trading Post store.

May 12, 1969
SLQ, AK

Hi Stan

Decide to answer your letters since you wrote twice, that you were coming this month so I didn't answer the other one. Anyhow we had breakup around the 2nd of May I guess, then it just stop and go etc. It went on like that until it was all gone. You remember those two drums down the beach front of my place, the water didn't even reach them, the water wasn't high at all.

Guess everyone is fine here plus you know what always be wrong with the peoples here, as usual including me sometimes. Just got your letter today. The boat didn't sink, in fact it didn't leak very much when we first put it in the water. All the snow melted, the ground was bare, then one morning when woke up it was all white, it snowed about 2-3", thats when I pull the boat down to the beach with the Skidoo, it was so easy to pull. Jack brought his down also.

My nephew Evan, Bernie and I went up to Holitna and camped one night, we had fun. You know that we used almost 4 boxes of shells (22) and didn't even hit one little duck. Bernie sure was having fun shooting away, even there so far away. Evan caught one beaver. It was a nice trip.

Also Mary and I went down to Georgetown yesterday for a visit and go see where it burned. There was a fire down there, they picked some guys from here, also from other places. One empty house burn down.

Oh it's getting green around here, grasses are starting to grow and everything else. There was two little fires here too. One started by Moxie Petes and the other one by Molgas today. There was three guys that came today

(over)

from getting riper, we were having a meeting, & was just three, all three of the pups went to sleep the first, no one of the crowd, the same, one of them was from the hospital, sanitation guy. He checked all the houses today. I'll tell you about it when you come back. I didn't finish yesterday. Anyway, mary came over this evening & she ask me to go with her down to Ed & self to the camp. Theres about 3 other couples there. Clara is all there is the camp too. We had a nice visit with some of those women. My pen can't seem to write very good. Oh, my needle works very good on the phonograph. Thank you! Does it really cost $0.95? I forgot to give you money for the egg beater. So, I'm sending you $10.00, I love you 5¢ more for the needle, anyhow huh? When I told mary I had a letter from you, she tell me to read it while she was here, she was worried about your bills I told her I was going to pay for some of them for fixing my boat. That made her feel better. I told mary you were still looking for his bullets the he said you never find none. mary that you werent coming back. If you have time I also would like to get me 2 writing tablets, please, I am absolutely out. my handwriting is terrible, also my spelling. I think I better go back to school. Well, guess we'll be seeing you soon, huh?

Nattie

p.s. Better come fast, we need someone to run the projector. also, its lonesome forgot to tell you, I'm learning how to run the around here projector. But, we never had s more in a long time. without you.

from Stony river, we were having a meeting and was just (thru). All three of the guys went to fight the fire. None of the guys was about the (?). One of them was from the hospital, sanitation guy. He checked all the houses today. I'll tell you about it when you come back. I didn't finish yesterday. Anyway, Mary came over this evening and she ask me to go with her down to Red Devil to the camp. Theres (?) 3 or 4 couples there. Alans are there in the camp too. We had a nice visit with some of those women. My pen cant seem to write very good. Oh my needle works very good on the phonograph. Thank you! Does it really cost $10.95? I forgot to give you money for the egg beater, So I'm sending you $10.00, ok? I owe you $5 more for the needle, anyhow huh? When I told Mary I had a letter from you she tell me to read it while she was here, she was worried about your bills. I told her I was going to pay for some of them for fixing my boat. That made her feel better. I told Nixie you were still looking for his bullets, he said you never find none. Mary (thought) you weren't coming back. If you have time I also would like you to get me 2 writing tablets, please, I'm absolutely out. My handwriting is terrible, also my spelling. I think I better go back to school. Well, guess we'll be seeing you soon, huh?

Nattie

P.S. Better come fast, we need someone to run the projector. I forgot to tell you, I'm learning how to run the projector. but, we never had a movie in a long time. Also its lonesome here without you.

RETURN

Coming back was very interesting. The people of Sleetmute had kept my secret from VISTA, even though some thought that I wouldn't ever come back.

I had only been gone a couple of weeks but I returned to a different Sleetmute. It was spring, and spring in its own way was just as ferocious as the winter. With a sun that was staying out eighteen hours a day, the foliage grew continually. Everyday was a powerhouse of growth. Everything was becoming green.

The ice was gone. The river back. Life in the village was bustling. Everyone was out doing something.

After the winter, everything that survived, thrived.

We were all spring.

THE LAST SUPPER

The last night before I was to leave many people stayed up all night with me doing, of all things, talking. Talking! They asked me, among other things, questions about marijuana and modern art. We laughed about many of the things that had happened during the year. What was this all about? There was more conversation that night than in the whole year. Maybe they were just shy. Maybe it was *me* who wasn't talking all year.

Anyway, during the laughter, as I looked at all the faces around me I realized nobody had died in the village this past winter. I remembered a little conversation I had with myself, seemingly a million years ago. I knew I certainly couldn't take credit for anything….. but inside, I smiled.

When the dawn broke I finished my packing. This was it. I'm really leaving. There were some small good-byes. I boarded the mail plane. Another take-off but not the same. No. Not the same at all.

PRATT INSTITUTE

THE TRUSTEES OF PRATT INSTITUTE, BY VIRTUE OF THE AUTHORITY
VESTED IN THEM, AND ON THE RECOMMENDATION OF THE FACULTY,
HAVE CONFERRED ON

STANLEY W. RESNICOFF

THE DEGREE OF

BACHELOR OF INDUSTRIAL DESIGN

FOR SATISFACTORY COMPLETION OF THE PRESCRIBED COURSE OF INSTRUCTION
IN EVIDENCE WHEREOF, THIS DIPLOMA HAS BEEN AWARDED
IN THE BOROUGH OF BROOKLYN, CITY OF NEW YORK,
JUNE SEVENTH, NINETEEN HUNDRED SIXTY-EIGHT.

James B. Donovan
PRESIDENT

CHAIRMAN, BOARD OF TRUSTEES

DEAN, SCHOOL OF ART AND DESIGN

THE LETTER

The year was over. I had done it. I felt great.

Jim's report about me in Sleetmute was good. (Amazing!). It was so good in fact that VISTA offered me a position as an Area Coordinator in Alaska if I wanted to stay. I didn't. I was already basking in thoughts of the mythical Hawaii. The 'promised' land.

I'm waiting in my hotel room. A VISTA supervisor, Jack Prebis, is coming over to talk to me about my transfer to Hawaii. Wow! It's really happening. Jack arrives. We're sitting on the beds facing each other. "Stan", he says, "this has nothing to do with you personally..." Every sensory cell in my body is alerted. This probably ONLY has to do with me personally. He continued. "I know VISTA made some promises to you but the reason you can't go to Hawaii is that we need people there with special talents...they need a photographer, an industrial designer, an....."

Now when Jack said the words "can't go to Hawaii" my mind buckled. Jack was not talking to the kid they had sent to Sleetmute a year ago. He was talking to the Eskimo in me. I was mad. Eskimo mad. This was fuckin' government's gussach lies, I thought. If I had my gun I might have shot him...just as a warning.

But when he said the reason I wasn't going was because they needed an 'industrial designer', I cracked. I stood up while he was talking. (he stopped). I walked over to my army duffel bag and began emptying it, like an animal, throwing my possessions all over the room. Jack watched this display in silence. I just had to make sure. It had been a long year after all. Finally I found it – at the bottom. It was the very first thing I had packed because it was the last thing I thought I would ever need in Alaska. My diploma. I opened the little leather folio. I read it. I <u>was</u> an industrial designer.

I walked back over to Jack, holding the diploma up in the palm of my hand and held it up for him to read. Then with all the fury in my heart I pushed it <u>hard</u> into his face. Hard. He quickly left the room.

I'm left sitting on the bed fuming but crushed by this turn of events when I hear laughing. Peeking in from the next room was Roger, another VISTA Administrator, and he's actually laughing at this whole scene. I was ready to kill him with my bare hands but he approached me with his palms outstretched to calm me.

"Look – I saw the whole thing and I just gotta tell you a story." You can imagine that I was in NO mood for a story, but he continued. "Do you know who Ken Kesey is?" I nodded I did. Confused. "Well a couple of years ago Kesey and me worked together at the Oregon State Psychiatric Hospital. We were both orderlies. Ken was there to do research for a book that he was writing called 'One Flew over the Cuckoo's Nest.' I was there because I really needed the job. Kesey would secretly change patient's prescriptions and generally screw things up just to see what would happen. I kept warning him that sooner or later they'd catch him. He just laughed."

I still had no idea what this story was about or what it had to do with me, but Roger had my interest.

"One day Kesey got called into the office. They told him that they knew what he'd been doing and threatened him with jail before they fired him. As they were escorting him out of the building he yells to me, laughing 'They fired my ass!' 'I told you they were gonna get you,' I said. 'Oh-yea,' Kesey says, 'and by the way they said they wanna see you next." I got canned too. Just for being Kesey's friend.

I'm bewildered. Roger looks me straight in the eye and continued. "Look, you're right about this whole Hawaii thing but it doesn't matter. You've only got one chance to get what you deserve and that's to sit down, right now, and write the best letter that you've ever written, about what's just happened to you, and send it to everyone important you know." I was stunned.

Three days. I worked nonstop on the letter for three days. After Sleetmute, words, especially written words, came hard. They looked so permanent. And they were so important. Three days.

I sent it off. To Jack, to his boss, to the heads of VISTA Alaska and VISTA Hawaii, to the Governor of Alaska, the Senators and Representatives of my home state of New York and Alaska and Hawaii and finally to the President of the United States.

Several days went by. Then I got a call from VISTA Headquarters. I remember it well. "Stan! Stan! Good News! We've cleared everything up over here and guess what – You're gonna go to Hawaii! Yea! That's Great! Just what we all wanted! And hey Stan, just do us one favor OK? Yea..Well.. Uh..Just don't write any more letters OK?

"Sure" I said.

On August 20, 1970 I landed in Honolulu, Hawaii. It was paradise.

EPILOG

THREE WEEKS LATER

I got a letter from Nattie. Nick Fogey was dead. His boat had somehow gone over and he had drowned. The whole year flashed by. I crumpled up the letter and threw it down. But it had already broken my heart.

AFTERWORD

Remember the newspaper headline I mentioned on the day that I arrived in Alaska?

Well, one year later....

The Pittsburgh Press, Monday, June 29, 1970

For Championing Eskimo, Indian Land Claims

55 VISTA Volunteers Fired In Alaska

By WILLIAM STEIF
Scripps-Howard Staff Writer

Rumsfeld

WASHINGTON — Fifty-five volunteers working for VISTA —the domestic peace corps— have been shipped out of Alaska and dismissed because they championed the land claims of the Indian and Eskimo villages where they worked as community aids.

Basic reason for the ferment is the VISTA policy change announced in April by OEO Director Donald Rumsfeld. He directed volunteers to move away from organizing the poor toward the less political goal of rendering social services.

He also scrapped VISTA's policy of supporting occupational deferments for draft-eligible male volunteers.

Reprinted by permission of Scripps Howard From the Pittsburgh Press By William Steif

Did somebody say 'OIL'?

And did somebody say Rumsfeld?

POSTSCRIPT

Recently *Kirkus Reviews* reviewed 'Sleetmute'. They were very complimentary. They said it was "incredibly entertaining" and also said "Resnicoff's encounters fascinate not only because they introduce readers to a world few have ever seen, but also because he's a gifted storyteller. He channels his 24-year-old self's confusion and naïveté in a way that is by turns hilarious, endearing and often quite moving." Very nice.

But they also thought it fell short in three ways. First they said that I didn't say enough about what was going on in my life before Sleetmute, so I've added a brief introduction. I think they were right. I think it helps. Secondly, they said that it felt more like a collection of anecdotes rather than a full memoir. OK, but it *was* a collection of anecdotes. The truth is that the full story of my year was in those hours and days between the anecdotes. The quiet times of tea with someone. The waiting for the mail to be distributed and the laughter over something I can't recall now. I couldn't put that into words then. I still can't now

Finally they said that I didn't say enough about how my year affected me. I've thought a lot about it. There's no doubt that the people of Sleetmute did more for me than I possibly could have done for them. They helped me survive. Hey, if you ever need to know how to trap beaver, I'm your man. They gave me their friendship. And they also gave me a quiet confidence that I could endure anything. Priceless.

So I'll close with this little story. In the early 1980s I got a great job working for Mattel Toys designing educational games for computers. It was in California, near the beach, and I enjoyed what I was doing immensely. But no matter how great a job is, the best part is that two week vacation you get, and when mine came I loaded my dog and my camping gear up and headed north to Yosemite. I found a place in the woods, outside the park, far from the organized campsites with their electrical hookups and all that stuff. This site just had a place for a fire and nothing else. I was alone. I was tired after my drive. I threw up my tent, built a little fire, found a perfect "Y" shaped dead branch to use to prop up my coffee pot, threw some grounds in the water and laid back on my bedroll to get some rest.

At dusk approached I saw a rather big guy walking out of the woods towards me. I later found out that he was a full-blooded Apache. He stood in front of my little campsite and said two words. "Nice fire".

ABOUT THE AUTHOR

After Sleetmute, Stan spent three warmer years in Honolulu designing creative educational materials for the children of Hawaii. He then accepted a fellowship at the Center for Advanced Visual Studies at M.I.T for work that he was doing on natural sensory playgrounds called 'Playcanos'. While in Boston he was also the exhibits designer for the Boston Children's Museum, and later he designed creative learning games and experiences for the American Museum of Natural History (NY), the Bronx Zoo and the Smithsonian Institution.

In 1982 he joined Mattel Toys as an educational software designer eventually becoming the Director of their 'blue-sky' toy research group. He designed the award winning GeoSafari CD-ROM series. More recently, his first children's book, 'Stanley, the Seal of Approval' was published by Random House and it, as well as several other of his children's books and movies are now available online.

He lives in Redondo Beach, California.

www.StanResnicoff.com

Made in the USA
Las Vegas, NV
16 April 2021

21479695R00090